Prentice Hall
is an imprint of

Harlow, England • London • New York • Boston • San Francisco • Toronto • Sydney • Singapore • Hong Kong
Tokyo • Seoul • Taipei • New Delhi • Cape Town • Madrid • Mexico City • Amsterdam • Munich • Paris • Milan

PEARSON EDUCATION LIMITED

Edinburgh Gate
Harlow CM20 2JE
Tel: +44 (0)1279 623623
Fax: +44 (0)1279 431059
Website: www.pearsoned.co.uk

First published in Great Britain in 2011

Pearson Education is not responsible for the content of third party internet sites.

ISBN: 978–0–273–74557–0

British Library Cataloguing-in-Publication Data
A catalogue record for this book is available from the British Library

Library of Congress Cataloging-in-Publication Data
MacBride, P. K.
  Sage accounting in simple steps / P.K. MacBride.
      p. cm.
  ISBN 978-0-273-74557-0 (pbk.)
1. Accounting. I. Title.
  HF5636.M33 2011
  657--dc22

                                      2010052030

All photos featured are the author's own.

10 9 8 7 6 5 4 3 2 1
15 14 13 12 11

Designed by pentacorbig, High Wycombe

Typeset in 11/14 pt ITC Stone Sans by 30
Printed and bound in Great Britain by Scotprint, Haddington.

Sage Accounting

in **Simple** steps

P.K. MacBride

Use your computer with confidence

Get to grips with practical computing tasks with minimal time, fuss and bother.

In Simple Steps guides guarantee immediate results. They tell you everything you need to know on a specific application; from the most essential tasks to master, to every activity you'll want to accomplish, through to solving the most common problems you'll encounter.

Helpful features

To build your confidence and help you to get the most out of your computer, practical hints, tips and shortcuts feature on every page:

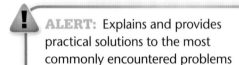 **ALERT:** Explains and provides practical solutions to the most commonly encountered problems

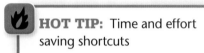 **HOT TIP:** Time and effort saving shortcuts

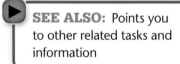 **SEE ALSO:** Points you to other related tasks and information

 **DID YOU KNOW?** Additional features to explore

WHAT DOES THIS MEAN?
Jargon and technical terms explained in plain English

Practical. Simple. Fast.

 in Simple steps

Author's acknowledgement:

Thanks to Sage, especially to their press office and support staff, for their help in producing this book. Thanks also to Joli Ballew for editorial advice and to Conor Temblett for finding the cover image.

Contents at a glance

Top 10 Problems Solved

Contents

4 Report Designer

5 The Company module

6 Double-entry book-keeping

7 Working in the Bank module

8 Customers and suppliers

9 Invoices

10 Credit control

11 Financial control

12 Products

13 Help and support

Top 10 Sage Accounting Problems Solved

Top 10 Sage Accounting Tips

Tip 1: Enter text

For the most part, the standard Windows data-entry and edit techniques work here as elsewhere, i.e. type in your text, using backspace to rub out errors and the arrow keys to move around within text. However, there are also a few special techniques that are worth knowing about, as they will enable you to enter data more accurately and quickly.

Almost all text that you write into the accounts will be short items – names, addresses and other details of new customers, entries on invoices, etc. Each of these items will normally go into a separate field (text box) on screen.

- If you have something that you want to spread over several lines, such as the details in a service invoice, press Enter at the end of each line.

- When you want to go to the next field, press Tab.

- If you need to go back to a field to correct an entry, hold down Shift and press Tab.

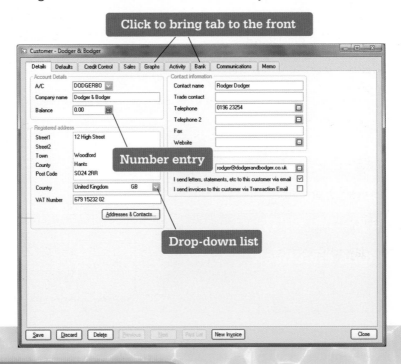

Click to bring tab to the front

Number entry

Drop-down list

❓ DID YOU KNOW?

The Customer record is a typical data-entry/display window. Most of these are tabbed windows – click on the label to bring its tab to the front.

Tip 2: Enter numbers and dates

Sage 50 provides easy ways to enter numbers, dates and any information that is already in your files.

- With number fields, you can call up a calculator. This can be very useful.

- For dates, the Program Date (normally the current date, but see page 8) is entered automatically into date fields. You can enter a different date if required.

1 Click on the calculator icon by the side of the field. A small calculator will appear.

2 Click on the digits to enter a number or use it as a calculator to work out discounts or other values.

3 Click the Backspace button if you need to correct a mis-key.

4 Click the = button to write the result into the field and close the calculator.

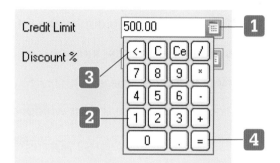

5 Click the calendar icon to open the calendar display.

6 Click to go to the previous year or ...

7 ... the previous month.

8 Click for the next year or ...

9 ... the next month.

10 Click on the day to select it.

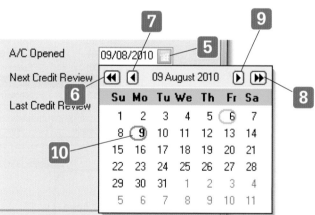

> **!** **ALERT:** The dates in this example appear in Day/Month order; elsewhere in the system you'll sometimes find them in Month/Day order.

> **🔥** **HOT TIP:** Press Esc or click elsewhere on the screen to close the calendar without changing the date.

Tip 3: Draw data from drop-down lists

If the data is already in the system, you can normally pick it from the drop-down list beside a field. This may be a short and simple list of codes, or a much larger set of data drawn from customer, supplier, product or other records. These record-based drop-down lists have extra features.

1 Click the arrow to drop down the list.

2 Click on the item to select.

3 Click on the arrow to display the list.

4 Use the slider to scroll through.

5 Select the item.

6 Click on OK to close the list window.

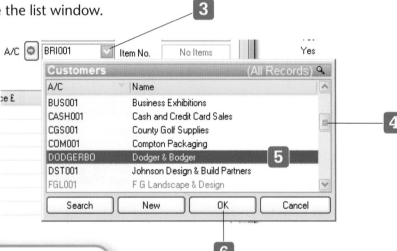

DID YOU KNOW?
In a record-based list, if it does not have the item that you want, you can click on New to create the record.

HOT TIP: When you are creating an invoice, simply picking the customer reference from a list pulls all the relevant address details into the invoice.

SEE ALSO: The same Search routine is used in many places in Sage 50. You can read about it on page 125.

Tip 4: Use a wizard

Wizards are there to guide you through the trickier routines. You will meet them when you first set up Sage 50, whenever you create a new customer, supplier or other account, when you are doing transfers within your Nominal Ledger, and in similar situations. They help to ensure that you supply the right kind of information and that it goes into the right place. Here's the New Customer Wizard as an example.

1 Select Customers in the navigation group to display the Customer List.

2 Click the New toolbar button to start the wizard.

3 Read the prompts and enter information or select optional settings where indicated.

4 Click Next to go on to the next panel.

5 If you want to correct an error, click Back to return to the panel.

6 If you decide to abandon the operation, click Cancel.

7 If you are not sure what to do at any stage, click Help.

8 At the last panel, click Finish to save your information.

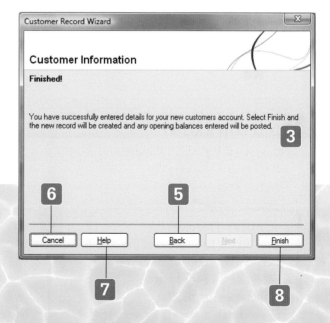

Tip 5: Create a user

Each person who is going to enter data into the system, or draw information out of it, needs to be set up as a user. To do this you need to create a name and password, and set their access rights. Some people will need access to the whole system, others may need to be able to get into certain areas only, e.g. the person who writes the invoices may have nothing to do with credit control.

1 Open the Settings menu and select Access Rights.

2 At the User Access Rights dialogue box, click New.

3 Enter the user's name and a password.

4 Select Full Access.

5 Click Save.

6 Repeat steps 3 to 5 to add other users as needed – you can add more at any time.

7 Click Close.

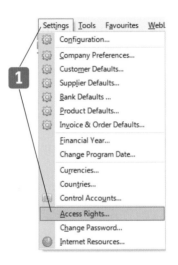

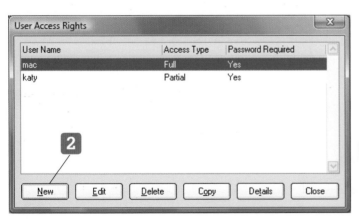

ALERT: This gives the user access to all areas of the accounts. If required, you can set limits on a user's access rights – see page 39.

HOT TIP: A password should be something that the user can remember but other people will not be able to guess. Your birthday, car registration number, the name of a child/pet/girlfriend/husband/etc. are not sensible ideas. Mixed letters and numbers are good.

Tip 6: Set defaults

Defaults can be set for all types of records and are then applied when new ones are created. Here's how to do it for customers' accounts. They should be set to the most commonly used VAT code, nominal code (N/C), department (if any) and discount rate. Most of these can be set by selecting from a drop-down list.

1 Use Settings, Customer Defaults to open the Customer Defaults dialogue box.

2 Start on the Record tab.

3 Use the drop-down lists to set the default Tax and N/C codes.

4 Type in the default Discount percent, if applicable.

5 Click OK.

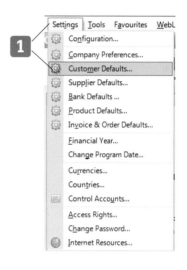

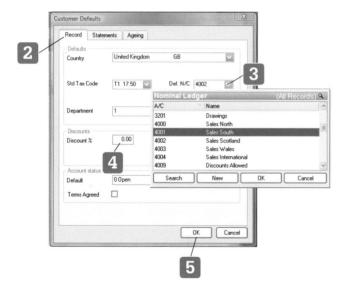

🔥 **HOT TIP:** The Statements panel simply holds the descriptions to be applied to invoices, credit notes and other printouts. You can probably leave this as it is.

Tip 7: Change the program date

Whenever a date is required, the current date will be set as the default, but it can be easily changed. If you intend to process a lot of transactions with the same date – and not today's – set the Program Date before you start.

1 Open the Settings menu and select Change Program Date.

2 Set the date by typing or by using the calendar display.

3 Set the date and click OK.

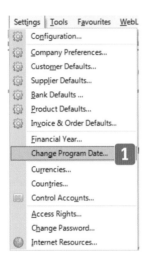

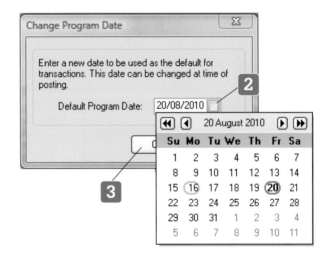

ALERT: The first rule of good book-keeping is to process transactions as soon as possible after they have occurred. Use this facility to catch up after a holiday or illness has created an unavoidable gap, not to make up for poor book-keeping habits.

HOT TIP: The program date will often need to be changed when you carry out month-end and year-end routines.

Tip 8: Set a password

If you need to protect your accounts, you can set a password to be given at the start of a session. The password should be something you won't forget but one that others will not guess easily. It should be changed regularly for optimum security.

1 Open the Settings menu and select Change Password.

2 If a password is already set, you will be asked for it before the routine will start.

3 At the dialogue box, type the password twice – as only asterisks are shown, this avoids mistyping errors.

4 If you make a typing error, or change your mind, click Discard to restore the original password.

5 Click OK.

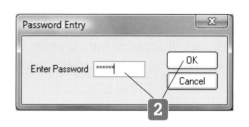

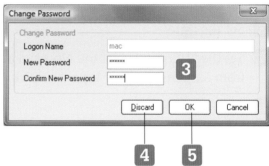

ALERT: The Sage system is not case-sensitive – LETMEIN, LetMeIn and letmein would all work if that was the password.

HOT TIP: If things change and a password is no longer needed, run the Change routine again and leave the Password fields blank.

Tip 9: Make a journal entry

A journal entry is a transfer between Nominal accounts. Typical uses include relocating amounts placed in Suspense, and recording depreciation or the revaluation of stock or other assets.

Making a journal entry is one of the few situations where you have to do the double-entry book-keeping yourself rather than leaving it to the system. An entry normally consists of a pair of transactions, one debit, one credit. Sometimes there will be more than two, but the total debits and credits must always balance – you cannot save the entries until it they do.

1 Click Journals to open the Nominal Ledger Journals window.

2 Give a Reference to identify the journal.

3 Set the Date.

4 Set the N/C number of the Nominal account into which the value will be moved from Suspense – either type it or pick it from the drop-down list.

5 Type the Details.

6 Enter the amount in the Debit or Credit column – this should be the same side as the original amount which produced the Suspense balancing entry.

7 Repeat steps 4 to 6 for the balancing entry to move the amount out of the Suspense account – this will be the opposite debit/credit to the original.

8 If there are several opening balances to correct, repeat steps 2 to 7 for each of them.

9 Click Save. If the total debit and credit entries are not the same, you will be alerted. You can save and exit from the Journals window only when the entries balance.

HOT TIP: Before you start, make a note of the details of the monies to be moved – the source and target accounts, date, reference and amount.

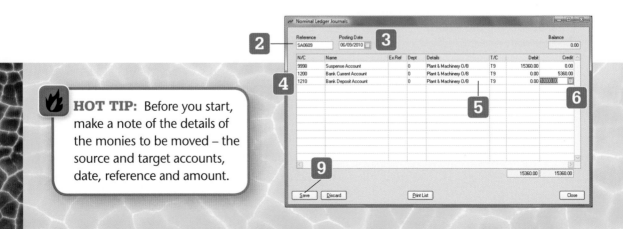

Tip 10: Use graphs effectively

Graphs can help to show underlying trends that are not immediately visible from the raw data. With the right sort of graph – bar chart, pie chart, line, scatter or Hi-Lo graph – presented in the right way, you can see relationships and changes over time much more clearly than you can by poring over sets of numbers. But beware – you can spend an awful lot of time trying out different display modes and tweaking the layout and design – and not have much to show for it at the end of the day.

1 Switch to the Graphs tab.

2 Click the Options button.

3 Tick to select the data sets – Invoices, Credits and Balances – to include in the graph and click OK.

4 Click the Graph Type button and select a type.

5 Experiment with the tools to see what they do and find settings that you like.

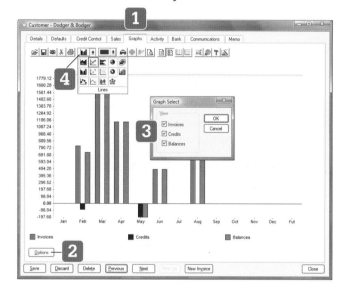

The toolbar buttons

Working across left to right, the buttons are:

- Open saved graph
- Copy data
- Colours

- Save as a chart file
- Print
- 3-D

- Copy image
- Chart type
- 3D View properties

- Z-clustered series
- Series legend on/off
- Titles
- Properties

- Zoom
- Vertical grid
- Format titles

- X-axis legend on/off
- Horizontal grid
- Tools

? DID YOU KNOW?

The Copy image tool captures the graph as a picture. It can then be pasted into a graphics application, or into a word-processed document as an image.

The Copy data tool copies the figures on which the graph is based. They can then be pasted into a spreadsheet or into a table in a word processor. Just to confuse you, the icon is used for the Cut operation in other Windows applications!

1 The Sage 50 system

Introduction

This chapter covers the essential techniques for working with Sage 50 Accounts. You will learn how to get started, and how to exit properly, how to find your way around the screen and how to adjust the display, how to enter and edit text, numbers and dates. Many of these techniques are the same as, or very similar to, ones you will have used with other Windows applications, so you can get to work with Sage 50 quickly, but there are a few significant differences which you need to be aware of from the start. Make sure that you understand the techniques covered in this chapter before using Sage 50 to work on the company's accounts.

Most Sage operations are straightforward and require no special knowledge. When recording sales, payments and stock movements, all that is really essential is that it is done accurately. With some operations, especially those concerned with setting up the accounts and the month- and year-end procedures, some understanding of book-keeping is necessary – for a start, you have to know your debits from your credits. This book will cover some of the theory behind operations when it is relevant, but it is no substitute for a proper training in accountancy.

Getting started

When you start Sage 50, you will be offered three choices. If you are new to Sage, tackle them from the bottom up:

- Open Demonstration Data. Use this to explore the system and see what it can do.

- Open Practice Data. This starts off empty. Build a simple, dummy company here so that you can get the feel of the key routines.

- Open Your Company's Data. Select this when you are ready to start using Sage 50 in earnest.

1 Select the mode.

2 Click on OK.

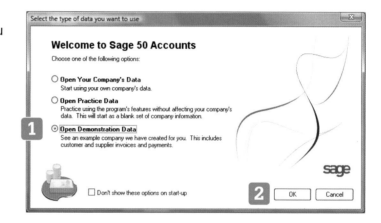

 HOT TIP: When you are using Sage 50 with your own company data, any time that you have to tackle something new, switch to the demonstration or practice data and try it there first. We all make mistakes when we are learning new things – so make them where it doesn't matter.

 ALERT: Once you are comfortable with the system, tick the Don't show these options on start-up tickbox so that you can go straight into work mode. You can get to the Practice and Demonstration data from within Sage 50.

Log on

The first time you log on, use the name 'manager' – there is no password. If you are the only person who will be using the system and your PC is secure, you can skip the log on. If several people will be working on the accounts, they will need to log on and each will need a user name.

With a new installation, before it has been set up for your company:

1 Enter the user name – 'manager' if it is a new system.

2 Click on OK.

Logging on with a user name and password:

3 Enter your user name.

4 Enter your password.

5 Click on OK.

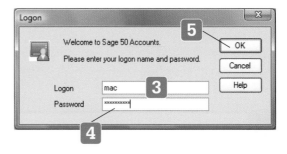

ALERT: If no one but you works on the accounts, but other people can access your PC, you should protect your precious company data. The user name could be left at 'manager', but you should at least add a password.

SEE ALSO: You can find out more about controlling access at the end of this chapter, and how to create users in Chapter 2. Use the manager logon while you find your way around the screen and the key routines.

Find your way round the screen

For anyone who has used Windows – and that must be almost everyone – much of the screen display and the way you interact with it will be immediately obvious. However, the system does have a few little wrinkles all of its own.

- The display area occupies the most space. It is mainly used for listing and selecting records. Data entry and display of transaction details are normally done in dialogue boxes or in separate windows.

- The tools above the display area vary to suit the contents.

- Buttons for common record-management jobs will be present in the display area if it contains a list.

- If several lists are open at the same time, each will be identified by a tab at the bottom of the display area. Click on a tab to bring its list to the front.

- The navigation bar occupies the left of the window.

- The Customers, Suppliers, Company, Bank and Products buttons are used to navigate between the groups of operations. They can be shown in full, with text labels, or as icons only on the bar beneath.

- The Tasks list shows the tasks that are directly related to the current navigation group. Some of these will produce lists in the display area, others will open dialogue boxes or new windows for data entry or analysis.

- The Links list leads to operations that are in both the current and other navigation groups.

View records

The record of an active account will contain a number of transactions, but its current status can normally be summarised in a single figure. The records of transactions, such as invoices, may also have several levels – an invoice may have a number of items, some of which may not have been paid for yet, or may have been returned, etc. Sometimes you want the simple summary, other times you want to 'drill down' deeper into the record.

1 In most lists, you will see a Record button in the toolbar. Click this to open a window to display the currently selected record.

2 If several records are selected, you will see the first. Click Next to bring the next one into view.

3 In the Customer and Supplier records, details of invoices are stored on the Activity tab. Click on this to bring it to the front.

4 To display the details of an invoice, double-click on its summary line.

5 If you see an arrow icon beside an item, you can click on this to display the details of the item.

6 You can often add notes here, and change the details if the transaction has not yet been taken into the system. Click OK to save any changes.

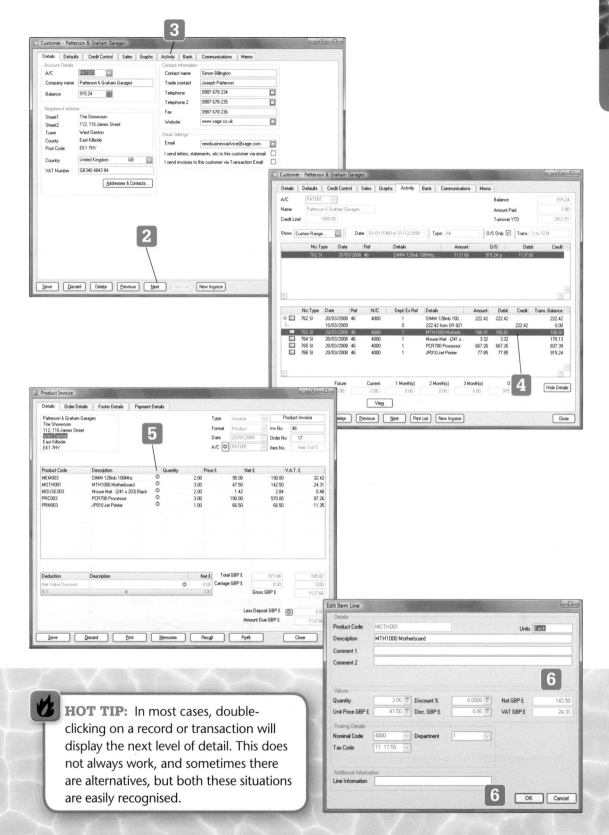

Adjust the screen display

You can adjust the width of the navigation bar and the depth of each of its sections.

Adjust the width

1 Move the pointer over the dividing line until it changes to a double-headed arrow.

2 Click on the line, hold down the mouse button and drag the guideline in or out.

3 Release the mouse button.

Change the depth of a section

4 Click on the handle at the top of the section.

5 Drag it up or down as required.

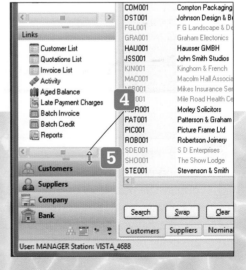

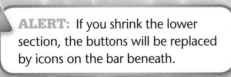

ALERT: If you shrink the lower section, the buttons will be replaced by icons on the bar beneath.

Alternative views

Some modules have alternative displays. The Customers, Suppliers, Company and Products modules have a Dashboard view, which shows graphs or text summaries of key aspects of the accounts. Customers and Suppliers also have a Process view, which offers an alternative way to the Tasks for starting jobs.

1 If there are alternative views, there will be a Change View button at the top right. Click on it.

2 This is the Dashboard view in the Customer module. Click Change View again to return to the normal display.

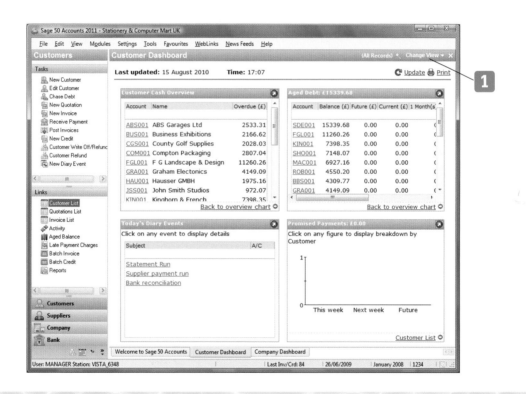

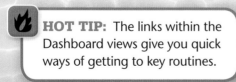

HOT TIP: The links within the Dashboard views give you quick ways of getting to key routines.

Enter text

For the most part, the standard Windows data-entry and edit techniques work here as elsewhere, i.e. type in your text, using backspace to rub out errors and the arrow keys to move around within text. However, there are also a few special techniques that are worth knowing about, as they will enable you to enter data more accurately and quickly.

Almost all text that you write into the accounts will be short items – names, addresses and other details of new customers, entries on invoices, etc. Each of these items will normally go into a separate field (text box) on screen.

- If you have something that you want to spread over several lines, such as the details in a service invoice, press Enter at the end of each line.

- When you want to go to the next field, press Tab.

- If you need to go back to a field to correct an entry, hold down Shift and press Tab.

Click to bring tab to the front

Number entry

Drop-down list

? DID YOU KNOW?
The Customer record is a typical data-entry/display window. Most of these are tabbed windows – click on the label to bring its tab to the front.

Enter numbers and dates

Sage 50 provides easy ways to enter numbers, dates and any information that is already in your files.

- With number fields, you can call up a calculator. This can be very useful.

- For dates, the Program Date (normally the current date, but see page 48) is entered automatically into date fields. You can enter a different date if required.

1 Click on the calculator icon by the side of the field. A small calculator will appear.

2 Click on the digits to enter a number or use it as a calculator to work out discounts or other values.

3 Click the Backspace button if you need to correct a mis-key.

4 Click the = button to write the result into the field and close the calculator.

5 Click the calendar icon to open the calendar display.

6 Click to go to the previous year ...

7 ... or the previous month.

8 Click for the next year ...

9 ... or the next month.

10 Click on the day to select it.

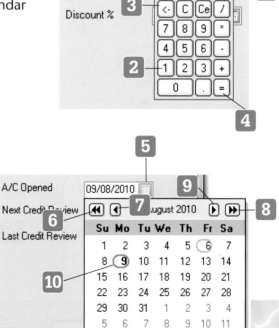

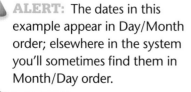

ALERT: The dates in this example appear in Day/Month order; elsewhere in the system you'll sometimes find them in Month/Day order.

HOT TIP: Press Esc or click elsewhere on the screen to close the calendar without changing the date.

Draw data from drop-down lists

If the data is already in the system, you can normally pick it from the drop-down list beside a field. This may be a short and simple list of codes, or a much larger set of data drawn from customer, supplier, product or other records. These record-based drop-down lists have extra features.

1 Click the arrow to drop down the list.

2 Click on the item to select.

3 Click on the arrow to display the list.

4 Use the slider to scroll through.

5 Select the item.

6 Click on OK to close the list window.

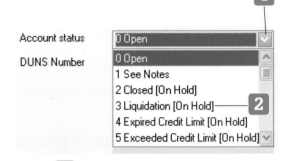

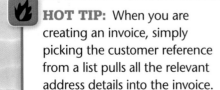

? DID YOU KNOW?
In a record-based list, if it does not have the item that you want, you can click on New to create the record.

HOT TIP: When you are creating an invoice, simply picking the customer reference from a list pulls all the relevant address details into the invoice.

SEE ALSO: The same Search routine is used in many places in Sage 50. You can read about it on page 125.

Select accounts

Before you can edit, delete or in any other way process a record or account, it must be selected. This is done by clicking anywhere on its line in its window.

Only one record can be selected at a time in the Bank and Financial modules, but in the Customers, Suppliers, Nominal, Products and Invoicing windows, any number of records can be selected at once, allowing you to process records in batches.

1 Click on the records you want.

2 If you want all but a few of the records, select the ones you *don't* want, then click Swap to invert the selection.

3 If you select one by mistake, click on it again to deselect.

4 If you have selected several then decide that you do not want them, you can deselect them all by clicking Clear.

ALERT: To select several records at once you do not need to hold down Ctrl as you do in most Windows applications.

ALERT: When a record has been selected it stays selected – until you deselect it. Before selecting records for deletion, first click Clear in case some off-screen records are selected.

HOT TIP: Multiple selection can be a real time-saver. For example, when you set up Sage 50 you need to enter opening balances for the Nominal accounts. If you first select all the relevant ones, you can then work steadily through the opening balances routine without having to constantly go back to select the next.

Use a wizard

Wizards are there to guide you through the trickier routines. You will meet them when you first set up Sage 50, whenever you create a new customer, supplier or other account, when you are doing transfers within your Nominal Ledger, and in similar situations. They help to ensure that you supply the right kind of information and that it goes into the right place. Here's the New Customer Wizard as an example.

1 Select Customers in the navigation group to display the Customer List.

2 Click the New toolbar button to start the wizard.

3 Read the prompts and enter information or select optional settings where indicated.

4 Click Next to go on to the next panel.

5 If you want to correct an error, click Back to return to the panel.

6 If you decide to abandon the operation, click Cancel.

7 If you are not sure what to do at any stage, click Help.

8 At the last panel, click Finish to save your information.

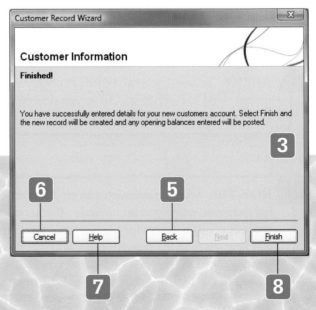

Smart links

Smart links offer a direct connection to related records. For example, when compiling an invoice, you may need to check or change some details in the customer's record. You could reach that record by going back into the main display, then opening it from the customer list, but there's a quicker way.

1 Next to the customer's account reference, there is a button with a fat arrow icon. This is a smart link.

2 Click on the smart link and the customer's record window will open immediately.

3 Use the tabs to get to the information you need.

4 Click Close to close the window.

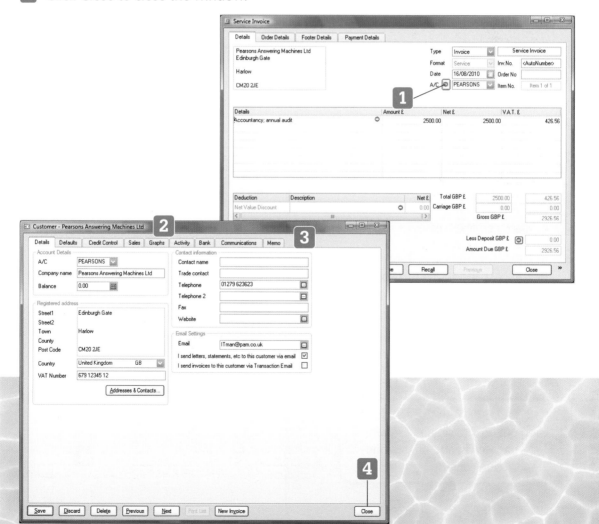

Single user? Multiple users?

The accuracy and integrity of your accounts are vital to the health of your business, so you must ensure that the only people who have access to the accounts are those who know what they are doing and can be trusted to do it properly. There are three levels of access control:

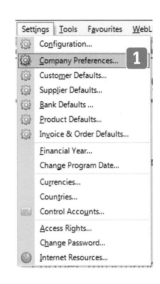

- Where the accounts are done by one person on one PC and the PC is secure, then you can turn off access control within Sage.

- Where there is only one user but the PC is not secure, you need to turn on access control and set a user name and password for that person.

- Where there are several users, you must turn on access control and each user must have a user name and password.

Whatever the situation, you need to set access rights early on because when Sage 50 is first installed, they are neither on nor off and this can create problems.

1 Open the settings menu and select Company Preferences.

2 Click on the Parameters tab to bring its panel to the front.

3 In the Others area at the bottom, tick Access Rights to turn on the user logon system, or clear the tick to turn it off.

4 Click OK.

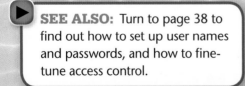

SEE ALSO: Turn to page 38 to find out how to set up user names and passwords, and how to fine-tune access control.

Shut down Sage 50

When you get to the end of a session with the accounts, you have three ways to end:

- If you have finished work on one set of data and want to start on, or carry on with, another, use File, Close – e.g. if you have been trying out a routine with the practice data. This will close the data files but leave Sage 50 running.

- If there are several users and another one may want to do some work, use File, Log Off.

- If you are the only person who works on the accounts, use File, Exit to shut down Sage.

1 Click to close the data files.

2 Click to log off. The Logon dialogue will appear, ready for the next user.

3 Click to shut down Sage 50.

Access Denied

User MANAGER is already logged in on machine Console_3596.

OK

ALERT: If no one wants to log on, when the dialogue box is closed, Sage 50 will shut down.

SEE ALSO: If a user does not log off, then next time they try to use the system they will be blocked by this message. There is a solution to this, but it's messy. See Problem 1, page 212.

2 Setting up the accounts

Introduction

The Sage system must be configured to your business before it can be used. There are two aspects to this: entering the basic details about the company and its bank accounts, and setting the defaults to be used in your customer, supplier and product records and in your invoices and orders.

You don't have to complete the configuration in one session, but to complete it you will need:

* if it is not yet activated, the software's serial number and activation key – you will find these in the pack

* your company's contact details, financial year start date, and VAT registration number

* the default credit terms, VAT code, nominal and department codes that will be used with customers, suppliers and products.

If you are new to Sage and will be using it for your own business's accounts, take the time to work through the procedures for setting up the accounts and for processing the common transactions using practice data. Don't go live with your own data until you understand how the system works. You do not need to master every detail – much can be learned as you go – but you do need an overview so that things make sense.

At this stage, skip the set-up routine – there's a dummy company set up already in the Practice data – and go straight to the Configuration Editor, then on to explore how Sage handles users, customers, suppliers and products.

Set up the company data

When you set up Sage 50, the wizard will create a basic set of Nominal Ledger accounts. But different types of businesses need different structures of accounts – a lawyer won't have retail sales or need to record products in stock, for instance, so pick the type of company which best matches yours at the My Company stage. The set of accounts won't be exactly as you want it, but it will be a good basis which you can then adapt to your needs.

1. At the Welcome screen, select Open, Your Company's Data and click OK. Or ...

2. Open the File menu, select Open, then Open Company Data.

3. The ActiveSetup Wizard will run. At the first stage, select Set-up a new company (unless you are importing existing data).

4. Enter your company details and click Next.

5. At Select Business Type, pick the type which is closest to yours – the Preview lists the main accounts. General is a good basis for most retail or wholesale businesses.

6. At My Financial Year, pick the month when your year starts.

7. At Select VAT Details, enter your VAT number. Select the option if you use the Cash Accounting scheme.

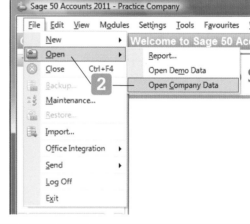

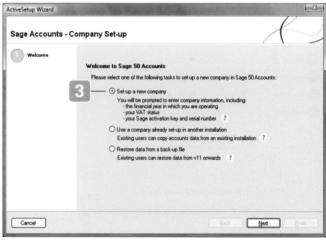

8 At My Currency, select the default currency used for billing.

9 At Activate Program, enter the software's serial number and activation key. If you have any problems with this, the phone line help desk is very good.

10 At the final stage, check the details. If you spot an error, use the Back key to return to the relevant stage to correct it, otherwise click Finish.

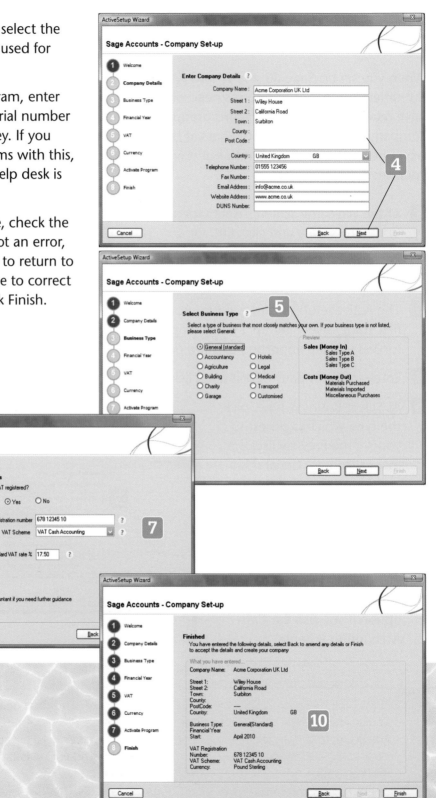

Set up the company template

During installation, you will have set up some of the details and defaults for your company, its customers, suppliers and products. Any information that was not entered then, or has changed since, can be put in through the Configuration Editor or the Company Preferences options. The initial set of nominal ledger accounts – the chart of accounts – is determined by the company template. You can pick a different company type on the General tab.

1 Open the Settings menu and select Configuration.

2 On the General tab, click Browse to open the Company Configurations dialog box.

3 Scroll through the list and select the most suitable template for your business.

4 Click Open to apply the template.

HOT TIP: To explore this using Practice data, either select Open Practice data at the Welcome screen or use File, Open, Open Practice Data.

ALERT: The chart of accounts created at this point gives you the basic structure of nominal accounts, grouped into categories. You can add to or adapt this to fit your business's needs.

Set up regions or divisions

If your company is organised into regions, and/or has several branches, and/or some other form of subdivision, these can be written into the Sage 50 system and used when analysing activity. Even if there are no actual divisions, it can be useful to set up 'virtual' ones for each area of the firm's work, as this will enable you to see more easily the relative profitability of each.

1 Switch to the Custom Fields tab.

2 Click into the first field under either Customers or Suppliers and replace 'Analysis 1' with a word to describe the subdivision, e.g. 'Region'.

3 For a second analysis type, click into the second field and type in the term, e.g. 'Branch'.

4 Repeat for a third type if necessary.

5 Click Apply to write the changes into the system.

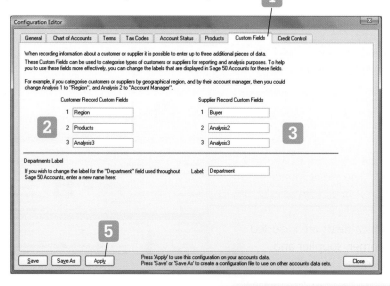

ALERT: The configuration that you set up through these tabs will apply to the practice or company data. If you want to apply it to other data sets, click Save or Save As and save the configuration as a file.

HOT TIP: Notice the Departments Label. Sage assumes that if the firm has subdivisions, these will be called 'departments'. If you use a different term, e.g. 'sectors', write that in here. The names for the departments are entered and edited through the Company module (see Chapter 4).

Set your Company Preferences

The Company Preferences dialog box has eight panels. It's worth looking through these now. In particular, check the Address and VAT details and the options on the Parameters and Budgeting panels.

1. Open the Settings menu and select Company Preferences.

2. On the Address panel, enter your contact details if they are not already there. These will be used on your letters and invoices.

3. On the Parameters panel, set the options as required.

4. On the VAT tab, check the settings and enter your details for online submissions.

5. On the Budgeting tab, leave the Method as Standard to have a basic monthly budget against individual nominal accounts, or change to Advanced and select the Type.

6. Click OK.

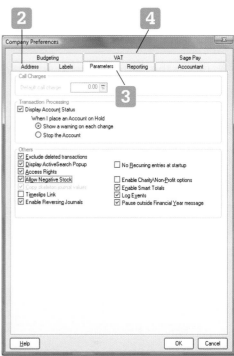

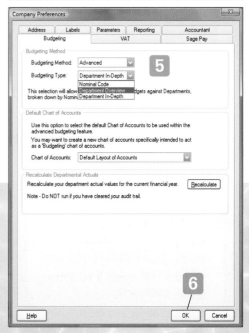

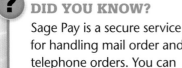

HOT TIP: The Labels panel is probably best left alone until you really know the system. This controls which fields are included in the customer, supplier and product records.

? DID YOU KNOW?
Sage Pay is a secure service for handling mail order and telephone orders. You can set up an account and enable the service from this tab.

Create a user

Each person who is going to enter data into the system, or draw information out of it, needs to be set up as a user. To do this you need to create a name and password, and set their access rights. Some people will need access to the whole system, others may need to be able to get into certain areas only, e.g. the person who writes the invoices may have nothing to do with credit control.

1 Open the Settings menu and select Access Rights.

2 At the User Access Rights dialog box, click New.

3 Enter the user's name and a password.

4 Select Full Access.

5 Click Save.

6 Repeat steps 3 to 5 to add other users as needed – you can add more at any time.

7 Click Close.

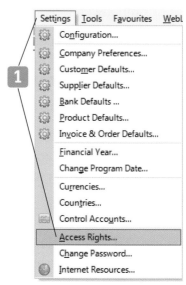

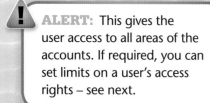

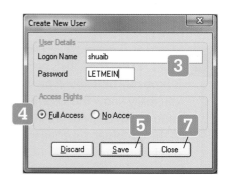

ALERT: This gives the user access to all areas of the accounts. If required, you can set limits on a user's access rights – see next.

HOT TIP: A password should be something that the user can remember but other people will not be able to guess. Your birthday, car registration number, the name of a child/pet/ girlfriend/husband/etc. are not sensible ideas. Mixed letters and numbers are good.

Set access rights

If people have different responsibilities, you may need to restrict their access to certain areas or to certain tasks within areas. Sage lets you set precise limits to access. You can control which modules people can access and even which dialogs within a module. The process is fiddly but should need to be done only once for each person – or once for each job specification.

1 Open the Settings menu and select Access Rights.

2 Select the user and click Details.

3 Click Modules.

4 Select the module(s), then select Full or Partial in the Access Type column.

5 Click OK to save the settings.

6 Click the + sign beside a module to see a list of its dialogs.

7 To set access at this level, select the module, then click Dialogs and set access as for Modules.

8 Click Close.

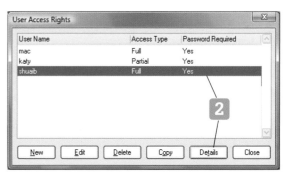

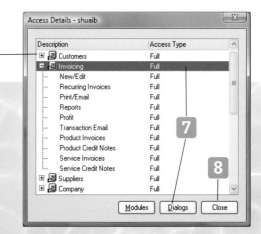

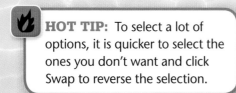

HOT TIP: To select a lot of options, it is quicker to select the ones you don't want and click Swap to reverse the selection.

Create users by copying

In the User Access Rights dialog box you will see Copy. Use this to create a user with the same access rights as an existing one. Even if the rights are not exactly the same, starting from a similar level will often be quicker than starting from scratch.

1 In the User Access Rights dialog box, select the user with the closest set of access rights.

2 Click Copy.

3 Enter the Logon Name and Password to create the user and click OK.

4 Back at the User Access Rights dialog box, select the copied user and click Details.

5 Make any necessary changes at module or dialog level.

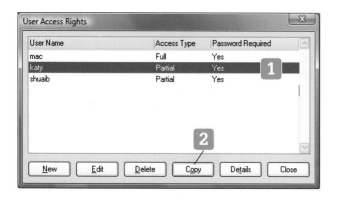

Set credit terms

The Customers and Suppliers defaults follow the same pattern – and some of the settings apply to both. Some are set through the Configuration Editor, some through the Customer and Supplier Defaults dialog boxes.

1 Use Settings, Configuration . . . to open the Configuration Editor.

2 Switch to the Terms tab.

3 What terms would you normally set for your new customers?

4 What terms do your suppliers normally set?

5 If relevant, tick Customer Finance Rates. To add a new rate, or change an existing one, click Add or Edit.

6 Set the date to apply from, and the rates, then click OK.

7 Switch to the Account Status tab if you want to define terms (see next page).

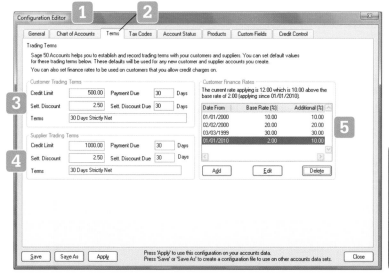

ALERT: Remember that these are only the default settings. When you are creating a customer or supplier account, you can change the settings as needed.

SEE ALSO: The finance rates are used when applying credit charges. See page 161.

Define account status terms

This provides a set of labels that can be attached to an account, but will almost certainly be of more use to more people. As well as showing the status of the account, these can be set to put an account on hold.

There are ten ready-made status descriptions, mostly relating to problem accounts, and these are all set so that the account is put on hold when the status is applied.

To change or create an account status:

1 Select the status to change, or an unused line to create a new status.

2 Click Edit.

3 Type a description.

4 If you want these accounts to be marked 'On Hold', tick the box.

5 Click OK.

6 Click Apply to fix the settings.

7 Click Close.

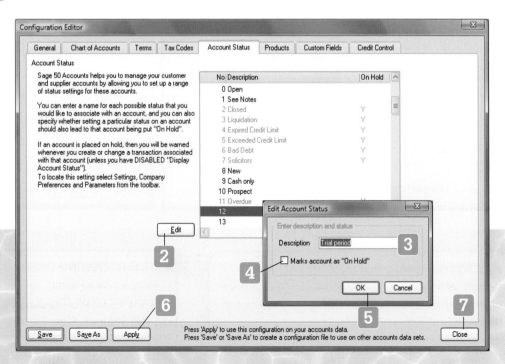

Set the customer defaults: Records

These defaults are applied to new transactions on customers' accounts. They should be set to the most commonly used VAT code, nominal code (N/C), department (if any) and discount rate. Most of these can be set by selecting from a drop-down list.

1 Use Settings, Customer Defaults . . . to open the Customer Defaults dialog box.

2 Start on the Record tab.

3 Use the drop-down lists to set the default tax and N/C codes.

4 Type in the default discount percent, if applicable.

5 Switch to the Ageing tab.

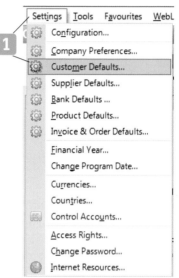

🔥 **HOT TIP:** The Statements panel simply holds the descriptions to be applied to invoices, credit notes and other print-outs. You can probably leave this as it is.

❓ **DID YOU KNOW?**
There is an identical Record tab in the Supplier Defaults dialog box. Use Settings, Supplier Defaults... to open this.

Set the customer defaults: Ageing

Chasing debts efficiently is a key part of good cash flow management. Aged Analysis groups overdue debts, with the default settings in multiples of 30 days. You can switch to calendar month grouping or set your own limits. At which point do you start counting? How old is a debt before you send a reminder, and how much older before you send for the lawyers?

1 If necessary, switch to the Ageing tab.

2 Select Calendar Monthly Ageing or Period Ageing.

3 If you select Period Ageing, check the limits for each period and change them if necessary.

4 Tick the box if you want to include future totals in balance.

5 Click OK.

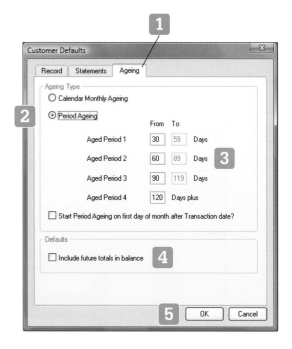

ALERT: There is an Ageing tab in the Supplier Defaults dialog box. Set this to match the terms of your main suppliers.

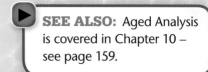

SEE ALSO: Aged Analysis is covered in Chapter 10 – see page 159.

Set the bank account defaults

Sage 50 comes with a basic set of bank accounts: current and deposit bank accounts, building society account, petty cash and company credit card. More can be set up if need be, and if you are likely to create more than a few, you may want to set the defaults.

1 Open the Settings menu and select Bank Defaults.

2 Tick the boxes to turn the options on or off to suit.

3 If you take money over the counter, check that the right nominal codes are selected in the Cash register settings.

4 If cash register takings are VAT inclusive, tick the box.

5 Click OK.

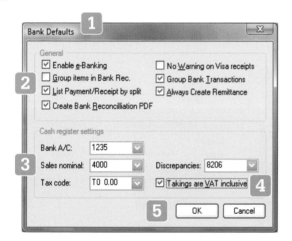

 SEE ALSO: You can find out how to create a new bank account on page 100.

ALERT: No Warning on Visa receipts turns off the alert that appears if a receipt is entered against a company credit card account.

? DID YOU KNOW?

List Payment/Receipt by split shows the individual transactions in an invoice. This is turned on automatically if the company uses VAT cash accounting.

Set invoice defaults

There are six settings tabs in the Invoice Defaults dialog box. All need to be checked and changed to suit your business. In particular, you should set the default invoice to the type you use most – product or service.

1 From the Settings menu, select Invoice Defaults.

2 On the General tab, set the default invoice and sales order format and their related options.

3 On the Footer Defaults tab, set the default net costs and nominal codes for carriage on sales and purchases.

4 On the Options tab, set the start points for numbering on the print-outs if you want to pick up from existing sequences.

5 On the Discounts tab, set the defaults for how and to whom discounts are to apply.

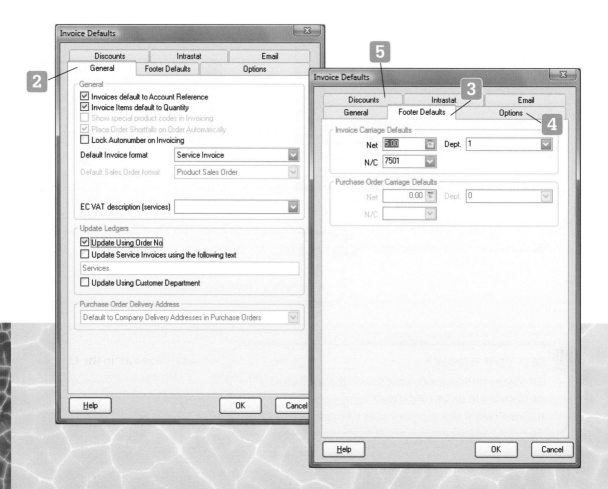

6 If you will be sending invoices by email, go to the Email tab to pick the layouts to use.

7 Click the Browse button and select a layout – there are some ready-made ones, but you may need to create your own layouts for these.

8 Click OK.

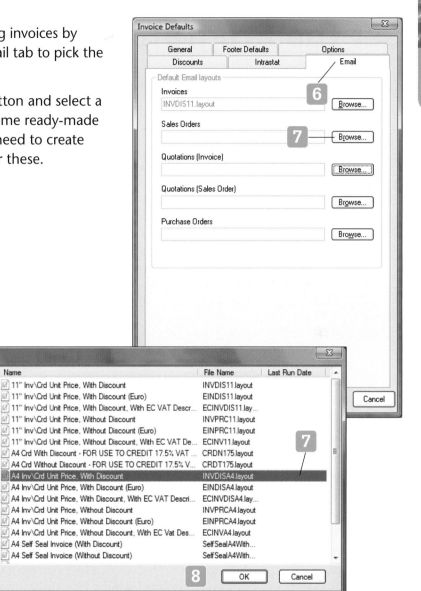

HOT TIP: If you have cash sales, you should select which print-outs are to be produced with each sale.

ALERT: If your trade within the EU requires it, switch to the Intrastat tab and turn on the reporting options.

Set the Program Date

Whenever a date is required, the current date will be set as the default, but it can be easily changed. If you intend to process a lot of transactions with the same date – and not today's – set the Program Date before you start.

1 Open the Settings menu and select Change Program Date.

2 Set the date by typing or by using the calendar display.

3 Set the date and click OK.

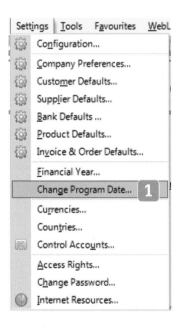

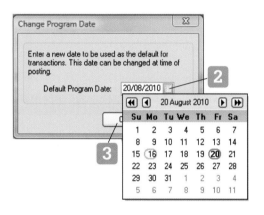

ALERT: The first rule of good book-keeping is to process transactions as soon as possible after they have occurred. Use this facility to catch up after a holiday or illness has created an unavoidable gap, not to make up for poor book-keeping habits.

HOT TIP: The program date will often need to be changed when you carry out month-end and year-end routines.

3 Looking after your files

Introduction

A company's data is its lifeblood. Accurate and securely stored records are essential to your company's health. You need to be sure that the information goes in accurately and promptly in the first place – and that's a matter of training and good working habits. You then need to be sure that the files are always in good order, that they are safe from interference, and that they are properly backed up so that the system can be restored in the event of a computer disaster.

Set a password

If you need to protect your accounts, you can set a password to be given at the start of a session. The password should be something you won't forget but one that others will not guess easily. It should be changed regularly for optimum security.

1 Open the Settings menu and select Change Password.

2 If a password is already set, you will be asked for it before the routine will start.

3 At the dialog box, type the password twice – as only asterisks are shown, this avoids mistyping errors.

4 If you make a typing error, or change your mind, click Discard to restore the original password.

5 Click OK.

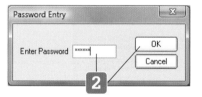

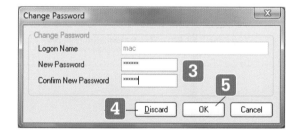

ALERT: The Sage system is not case-sensitive – LETMEIN, LetMeIn and letmein would all work if that was the password.

HOT TIP: If things change and a password is no longer needed, run the Change routine again and leave the Password fields blank.

File maintenance

All data needs a certain amount of maintenance to be kept in good order. Sage 50 has a set of commands to help maintain your data. Three of these should be used as a matter of routine – see the following pages.

1 Open the File menu and select Maintenance to display the File maintenance dialog box.

2 All the operations start from here – click on a button to start.

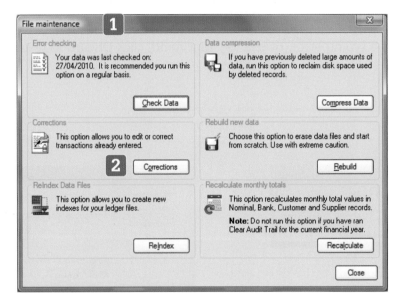

WHAT DOES THIS MEAN?

Reindex Data Files: Indexing allows a data file to be searched more efficiently, but reindexing is not to be undertaken lightly, as the process can damage the files! If you know that the files have undergone a lot of changes, and it seems to be taking ever longer to pull up records from the files, contact customer support and discuss reindexing with them before doing anything.

Rebuild new data: Not for normal use! This erases all your data files so that you can start again from scratch. Use it after you have been working with the dummy data to get the hang of the system, or possibly after a major crash and before a complete restore from backup.

Recalculate monthly totals: Another just-in-case routine. If your files have been corrupted and you have lost the monthly totals, this will recalculate them as far as possible from available data.

Check data

The Check data routine will scan your files, and the links between them, to make sure that your data is in good order. If all is well – and it almost certainly will be – you will get the Check Complete message.

1 Click OK to close the dialog box.

> ### WHAT DOES THIS MEAN?
>
> What if it's not OK? If things have gone awry, the File Maintenance Problems Report window will be displayed.
>
> **Summary:** Gives you an overview. To get the details of any errors, warnings or comments, switch to the appropriate tab. Errors are problems with the data that need fixing immediately.
>
> **Warnings/comments:** Normally relate to minor inconsistencies which you should be able to correct from within the system.
>
> **Fix:** This facility will correct most errors. If it can't, then the files are corrupted and should be restored from the backups (see page 59).

Make corrections

If an error is made when entering a transaction, or a transaction is cancelled after it has been entered into the system, you may be able to delete or edit it through the Corrections routine.

1 On the File maintenance screen, click the Corrections button.

2 Select the transaction and click the Edit Item button in the toolbar.

3 If the transaction has not been reconciled on the VAT return, it can be deleted – click Delete Item if you want to do this.

4 Edit the information in the Details area as needed. Note that Totals cannot be changed – you must edit the details of the transaction.

5 To edit the details of an invoice, select the item and click Edit.

6 Edit the Details and Amounts as needed and click Close.

7 Click Save to write the changes to the files. You will be prompted to confirm that you really want to do this.

8 Click Close.

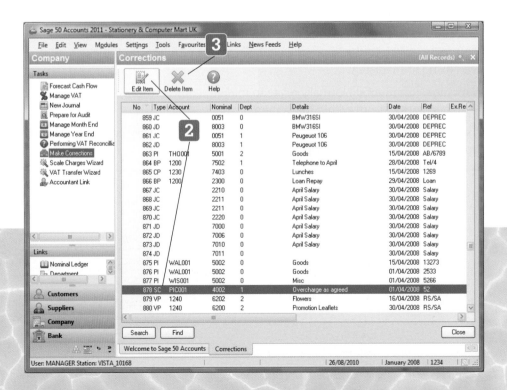

Number 878, Sales Credit Note

You can change details of all grouped items at once by using the fields below, or select individual transactions in the list to amend a specific item.

Sales Credit Note Details

Account PIC001

Reference 52

Description Overcharge as agreed   Posted by   MANAGER

Created on 12/08/2008

Posted on 13/09/2008   VAT Rec. Date 30/06/2008

Totals

Net 50.00   Tax 8.53   Paid 58.53

To edit details of a specific item on this Sales Credit Note, highlight the item and click 'Edit'.   Edit

Details   Net T/C   Tax
Overcharge as agreed   50.00 T1   8.53

Save   Close

Number 878, Sales Credit Note

Item Details

N/C 4002

Details Overcharge as agreed

Date 01/04/2008

Department 1

Ex.Ref

Project Ref

Amounts

Net 500.00   Tax 8.53   T/C T1 17.50   Paid 58.53

Flags

☑ Paid in full

Payment Allocations

Type	Date	Payment Ref	Details	Amount
SI	27/04/2009	42	58.53 to SI 712	58.53

Edit

Close

ALERT: Bank transfers (page 110) and journal entries (page 90) have matching double entries and cannot be deleted. You can edit only non-critical information, such as department codes and descriptive text.

HOT TIP: If you cannot correct the errors here, you can issue credit notes to nullify invoices or make journal entries to reverse mispostings.

Compress your files

When transactions and other data items are deleted – either through corrections or as part of clearing the audit trail (see page 185) – the data remains in the files but is flagged so that it is ignored by the system. The compression routine removes those records marked as 'deleted'. Do this from time to time to save disk space and to improve the efficiency of your data handling.

1 Open the File menu and click Maintenance.

2 Click Compress Data.

3 If you want to compress only certain files, clear the Compress All Data Files checkbox and select the required files.

4 Click Compress.

5 When compression is complete, click Close to exit the routine.

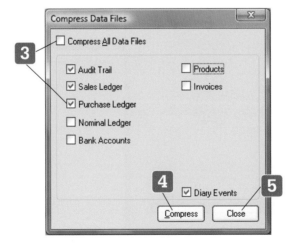

 ALERT: Always run the Check Data routine first (see page 53). If there are problems in the files, they should be found and fixed before compression.

Make backups

A good backup routine is essential. The Sage system is very reliable, but computers get stolen or damaged, and hard disks can fail. Would your business survive if it lost all its accounts data? How much data can you afford to lose and still survive? Backup files will store that precious data – and also hold your configuration settings and company details.

Backups should be made:

- daily, or possibly weekly, depending upon the number of transactions going through the accounts

- on removable media, stored away from the computer, in a fireproof safe, and preferably in another building

- with each backup on a separate disk or tape, so that if one is destroyed or corrupted, there is a recent previous version to work from. If you do daily backups, you may have a set of five (or six) that you recycle weekly.

1 Open the File menu and select Backup.

2 On the Backup Company tab, select the drive and directory, and edit the name as required.

3 On the Advanced Options tab, tick or clear the checkboxes to select the file types to back up.

4 Click OK.

5 Wait while the files are saved – this could take some time.

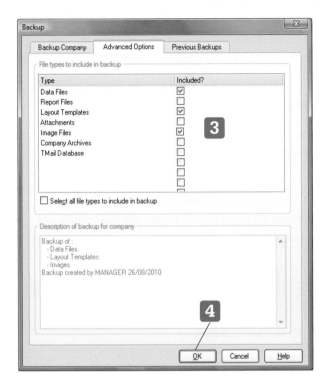

 ALERT: If necessary, you can cancel a backup part-way through – but you would have to start from scratch again later.

 DID YOU KNOW?

If you have not backed up recently, you will be prompted when you close down Sage 50. But don't wait for the prompt – get into the habit.

 HOT TIP: Before you start the backup, run the Check Data routine to make sure that the files are in good order (see page 53).

Restore files

If you have a computer failure or hard disk crash or suffer a destructive virus attack, you can recreate the files – if necessary on a new computer – using the Restore routine. You normally restore from the most recent backup, though you may have to use an earlier one if the files had been corrupted – without anyone noticing – at the time of the last backup (which is why you should check the data first).

1 Open the File menu and select Restore.

2 Click the Browse button and locate the backup file to use.

3 Click OK.

4 Wait while the files are copied back into place. This could take a while so you may as well take a break.

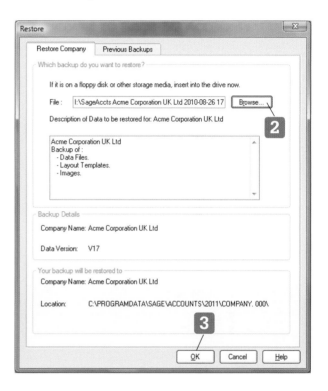

? DID YOU KNOW?

You will lose all the transactions that have been recorded since the backup, but if you have been maintaining the files properly and backing up regularly, they should not take long to re-enter.

! ALERT: Do not rely on the Sage backup alone. You should also back up your whole computer system regularly. If a Sage data file is seriously corrupted or erased, the program may shut itself down when you try to start it – which would prevent you from using the Restore routine within Sage 50. In this situation you would need to be able to restore files through the Windows backup and restore routines.

4 Report Designer

Introduction

Getting good quality information out of an accounts system is as important as putting accurate data in, and much of that information is produced in the form of reports. Sage 50 has a wide selection of ready-made letters, statements and other document formats which should be adequate for most accounting purposes. They are standardised, but if they are not quite what you need, you can edit them or you can create your own documents from scratch. The same Report Designer window opens whichever module you are in, and whether you are working on a label, letter, statement or report. The Report Designer can also be opened directly as a standalone program – you will find it in the Start menu in the Sage Accounts folder.

View a layout

You can create a report layout entirely from scratch, but it is normally simpler to start from one that almost does the job and adjust it to suit. Have a look at one to see how they are constructed.

1 In the Customers, Suppliers, Company or Bank module, click on the toolbar button for a report, letter or label.

2 At the Report Browser window, select the layout to use as a base.

3 Identify the elements of the layout.

The areas in a report

Notice the headings above each area. These vary and include:

- Report Header – anything in this area goes at the start of the report.

- Page Header – anything here will appear at the top of every page.

- Subsection Header – this features material to appear at the start of each account, department, category or whatever divisions apply.

- Details – this line is repeated for all transactions in each account.

- Footers – these are printed at the end of each account.

- Report Footer – this appears only on the last page of the report.

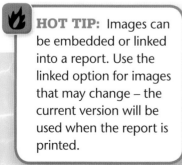

HOT TIP: Images can be embedded or linked into a report. Use the linked option for images that may change – the current version will be used when the report is printed.

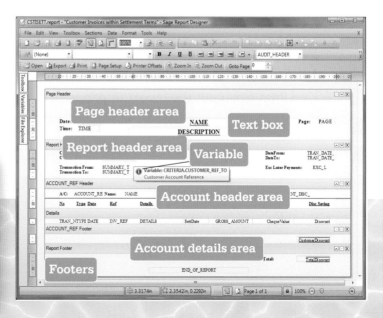

Produce a report

If there is a ready-made layout report which will do the job, you can quickly and easily produce a list of transactions or account summaries.

The Customers, Suppliers, Company and Bank windows have a Report toolbar button which will lead to a dialog box offering you a choice of ready-made report layouts. The reports are produced in PDF format and can be printed directly, or saved as a file, or attached to a message to send as an email.

1 Click the Reports button to open the Report Browser.

2 Select a set of reports in the left-hand pane.

3 Select a layout from the right-hand pane.

4 Click Preview to see how it will look.

5 With those reports that can draw on large numbers of records, you can set a range. Set the range of Customer Refs, or ...

6 ... the range of Transaction Dates, or ...

7 ... the range of Transaction Nos.

8 Give a number to see a sample in the preview, or leave this at 0 to see them all.

9 At the Preview window, use the Zoom and Goto Page tools to check out the preview.

10 Click Close.

11 Click on Print to output the report to paper, or ...

12 ... click on File to save it as a PDF file, or ...

13 ... click on Email to send it as an email attachment.

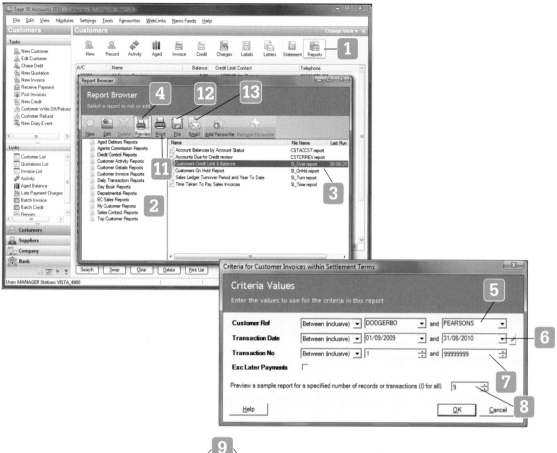

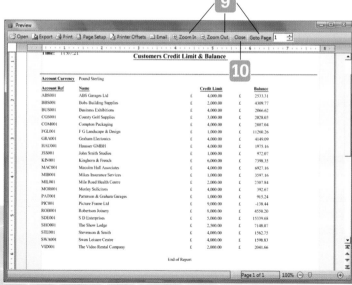

Print a set of letters or labels

It is almost as simple to print a set of reminder letters, or a batch of address labels for a mailshot. The only real difference here is that you need to select the recipients in the customers or suppliers lists before you go to the Report Browser.

1 Go to list view in the Customers or Suppliers module.

2 Select the people/companies for whom you want to produce letters or labels.

3 Click on the Letters or Labels button in the toolbar.

4 At the Report Browser window, select the layout to use.

5 There will be a delay while Sage draws data from the files and assembles the letters. Before the preview opens you will be asked whether you want to update the communication history. This is generally a good idea. Click on Yes.

6 Scroll through the previews, or use the Goto Page feature to check a sample of the outputs.

7 If all is well, click Print to output the letters, or ...

8 ... click on Close to return to the Report Browser window.

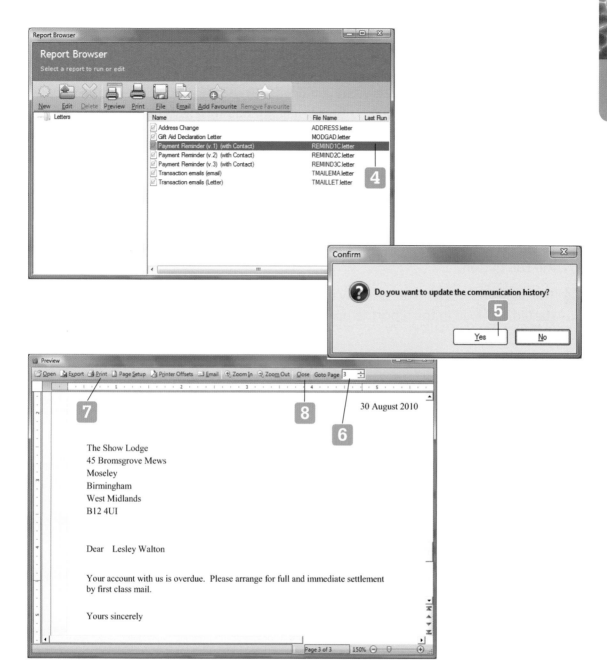

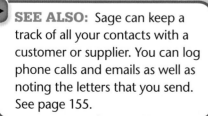

SEE ALSO: Sage can keep a track of all your contacts with a customer or supplier. You can log phone calls and emails as well as noting the letters that you send. See page 155.

? **DID YOU KNOW?**

The process is the same for labels as it is for letters, but with labels you are more likely to have to edit the layout – there are an awful lot of types of labels, and very few ready-made layouts.

Edit a report

If no ready-made layout is exactly what you need, it is usually much simpler to edit one of these than to start from scratch. This example is a reminder letter and we are adding the amount outstanding to the layout.

1. In the Customer module, select the customers to whom reminder letters are to be sent.

2. Click the Letters button.

3. At the Report Browser window, select a report, e.g. Payment Reminder v.1, and click the Edit button.

4. The Sage Report Designer window will open – it will take a few moments to get started and load in the report template.

WHAT DOES THIS MEAN?

A report layout can contain any of these elements:

Text: Written in separate boxes. If you start with a small box, it will expand as you type. The text can be formatted as in Word.

Lines and boxes: For marking off areas.

Images: Such as a company logo.

Variables: These draw data from your files.

Expressions: These can perform calculations on the data to work out costs, totals, days overdue, etc.

Barcodes: For use on product labels, etc.

5 Click the Toolbox tab, on the left of the window, to bring the Toolbox into view.

6 Click on the pin icon if you want to fix the Toolbox in place – it will close after use otherwise.

7 Try to identify the elements used on this layout.

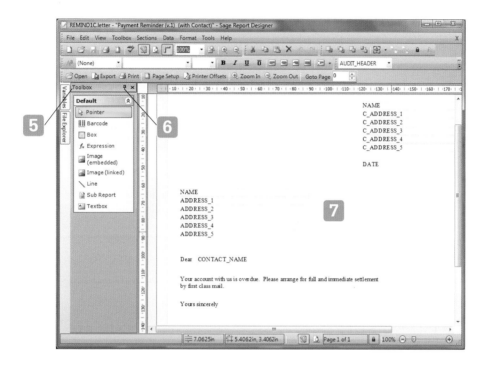

Add text

Text can be added anywhere on the report, but is written in text boxes. You can delete, edit or add to the text in any existing boxes.

1 Open the Toolbox and select the Textbox tool.

2 Click onto the report and drag a rectangle approximately where you want the text to appear.

3 To move a text box, drag on the four-headed arrow.

4 To change its size, drag on the handles on the corners and sides.

5 Type your text. If there is too much to fit, drag on the bottom or right edge of the box to expand it.

6 Click anywhere out of the box to end the text-entry mode.

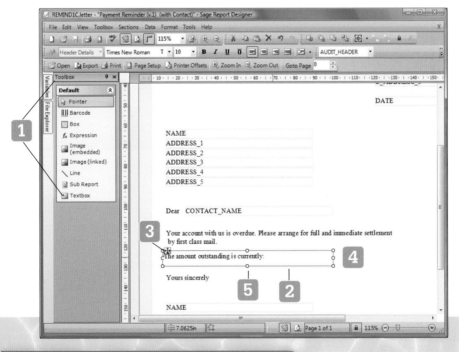

HOT TIP: The Report Designer has an automatic alignment feature. If you drag a text box (or any other element) when it gets to a place where it lines up with another element, one or two blue lines will appear to indicate the alignment.

Format text

To format the text, you must first select it.

1. To select some of the text within a box, click once in the box to make it active, then click and drag over the text.

2. To select all text in the box, click once on the box.

3. To select a group of boxes together, drag a rectangle that will cover or at least touch the ones you want.

4. Use the buttons and drop-down lists in the Formatting toolbar to set the font, size, emphasis or alignment, or …

5. Use the Style drop-down to apply a standard style to the text.

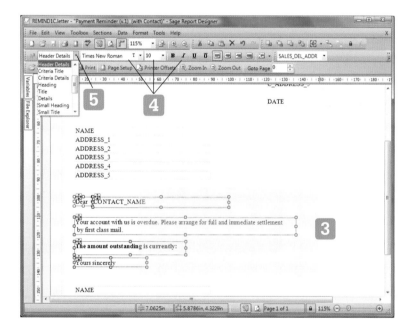

HOT TIP: Previewing before you print is always a good idea – especially when you have started from scratch. Things to check include:

- Are variable boxes wide enough to fit their data?
- Do variables line up properly with text in text boxes?
- Are any labels or headings spelled correctly?
- Is the spacing between boxes balanced?

Add variables

Just about any data that is stored in the accounts can be brought into a report using a variable. The tricky part is finding them! Variables are grouped by category and though the names are fairly obvious, it can take a bit of exploring to discover where everything is stored. In this case, we want to add the outstanding balance. This is in the Sales Ledger group and is called BALANCE.

1 Click the Variables tab on the left of the frame to display the Variables list.

2 Click the plus sign to open up the Sales Ledger group.

3 Locate BALANCE.

4 Drag the variable onto the report and drop it where you want the data to go. You can adjust its size and location later, if necessary.

5 Use the Formatting toolbar to format the variable as needed.

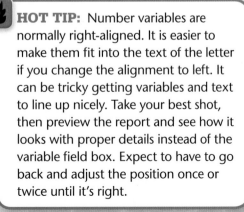

? DID YOU KNOW?

If you click on a variable, its full name is shown in the pane beneath the list, or if you point to it, its full name is shown in a pop-up. These can be useful with some variables, e.g. AGED_CUM_90, which is 'gross in first period and beyond (e.g. 30 days and older)'.

🔥 HOT TIP: Number variables are normally right-aligned. It is easier to make them fit into the text of the letter if you change the alignment to left. It can be tricky getting variables and text to line up nicely. Take your best shot, then preview the report and see how it looks with proper details instead of the variable field box. Expect to have to go back and adjust the position once or twice until it's right.

Add lines and boxes

Lines and boxes are useful for separating areas in a long report, or for making things stand out in a report or letter.

1 Click on the Line or Box tool to select it.

2 Click on the report where you want the line or box to start, then drag across to draw it. While you are dragging, the line or box will be shown in blue.

3 Use the four-way arrow handle to adjust the position if necessary.

4 Drag on a round handle at an end or corner to adjust the length or angle.

Where are the colour and line options?

If you are looking for line thickness options or colour palettes on the toolbar, you are wasting your time. You can change the line colour from the default black, but it's a bit fiddly. If you open the View menu and select Properties, the Properties panel will open on the right. Select any element on the report, and its properties – the things which control its appearance, behaviour, layout, etc. – will be shown here. Most properties can be edited, but many are best left well alone unless you really know what you are doing. If report design is important to you and you have the time, explore the Properties panel.

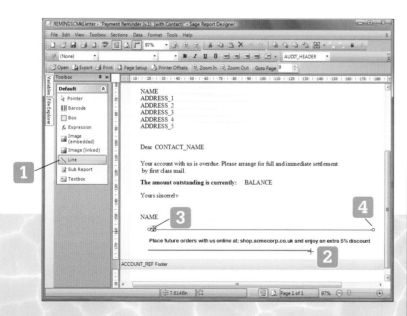

Adjust the page setup

You may want to change the margins as the defaults are small – around 6mm, or ¼ inch.

1 Click the Page Setup button, or open the File menu and select Page Setup.

2 In the Margins area, type in new values for the margins. Sage 50 normally uses millimetres.

3 If you have access to several printers, click the Printer button.

4 Drop down the list to select the default printer, then click OK.

5 Back at the main Page Setup dialogue, click OK.

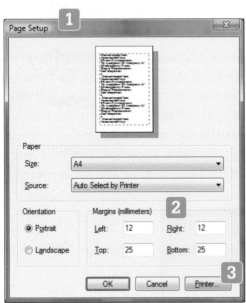

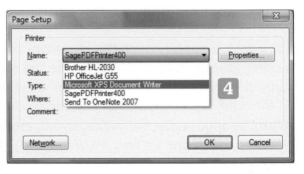

HOT TIP: You can change the units of measurement to inches or points in the Tools > Options dialog box.

DID YOU KNOW?
If you will normally output the report or letter to a PDF file, you can set the Sage PDF Printer as the default printer. When you start to print it will ask you for a filename and storage location.

ALERT: Don't forget to save your report design when you have finished – you'll need it later. Open the File menu and select Save As. Give it a name that will identify it clearly.

5 The Company module

Introduction

The Company module covers all of the Nominal ledger work, except for those tasks that relate to any of the bank accounts. Though the Nominal ledger is the heart of the accounting system, once it is set up there are relatively few situations in which you will work on it directly. The Nominal module is used mainly for viewing records, for performing (fairly rare) journal entries and for setting up budgets. It is here that you define the structure of the accounts, set opening balances, make journal entries and reversals, compile the VAT return and manage your assets.

The financial analysis tools and reports and the end-of-period routines can also be reached from this module.

View Nominal records

The record panels have four tabs:

- Details shows the current balance, and the balance, budget and prior-year figures for each month (if present).

- Graphs shows the same monthly figures in visual form.

- Activity shows the transactions currently in the audit trail for that account.

- Memo is a free space in which any notes can be written.

To view records:

1. Switch to the Company module. The Nominal Ledger will be open, showing a list of Nominal accounts.

2. If you want to look at a single record, double-click on it to open it.

3. If you want to look at several records, select them and click the Record button.

4. Click Previous or Next to move between the selected records.

5. Click on the headings to switch between the tabs.

6. Click Close when you've finished.

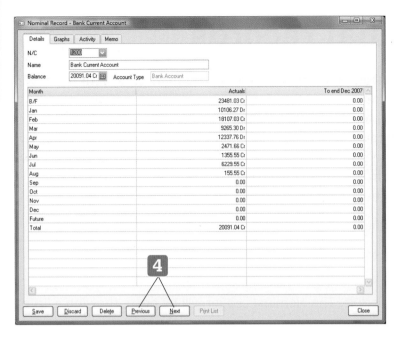

Budgets

If you want to include budget figures to help in analysing and monitoring your business's performance, they can be written into the Details tab of the Nominal Record window.

The budget data can be compared with the actual figures directly on the Details tab, or visually on the Graphs tab. The system can also produce a budget report, showing how far the actual figures differ from the budget, for the period and for the year to date.

To enter budget data:

1 Open the account in the Nominal Record window.

2 Enter a budget figure for each month – either type it in or use the calculator. Or ...

3 Enter a figure for the year and let Sage share this equally across the months.

4 Click on the Graphs tab for a visual comparison of the budget and the actual figures.

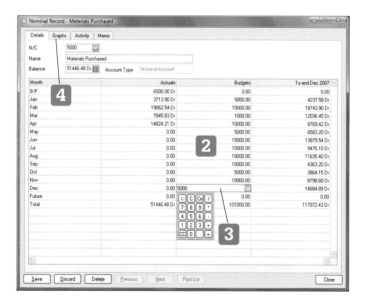

5 Use the Toolbar buttons to change the chart type, or to format its appearance.

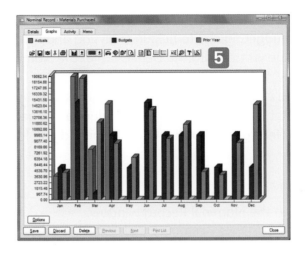

WHAT DOES THIS MEAN?

The buttons on the right of the toolbar all format the appearance of the chart in different ways. Have a play with them – you will quickly get the hang of them (though watch out for the 3D controls). The more useful tools are the first six. Working from the left, they are:

Import chart: Loads in a chart saved earlier.

Save chart: Saves the layout and options.

Copy the chart: Copies the chart as a bitmap image. This could be pasted into a report or a presentation.

Copy the values: Copies the figures from the Details tab. These could be pasted into a document or a spreadsheet. Weirdly, this uses the standard Windows Cut icon.

Print: Sends the chart to the printer.

Chart type: There are a dozen different chart styles to choose from.

 ALERT: The Budget column will be present if you have opted for Standard budgeting in the Company Preferences.

Edit the Chart of Accounts

The Chart of Accounts is used by the Sage 50 system when it draws up the Profit and Loss account (page 174) and the balance sheet (page 176). The default layout of the General configuration is outlined here. Accounts are grouped into category types, each of which has a number of standard accounts.

The Initial Range shows the nominal codes currently grouped in each category type. In some cases, there are substantial gaps in a range, e.g. with sales, the main group falls between 4000 and 4299, but there are then subranges for credit charges (4400–4499) and other sales (4900–4999), leaving big gaps where other categories could be inserted.

The Maximum shows the highest code that can be included in the category type – the next one is the first in another type.

Category Type	Initial range	Maximum
Fixed Assets	0010–0059	0999
Current Assets	1000–1250	1999
Current Liabilities	2100–2299	2299
Long Term Liabilities	2300–2399	2999
Capital & Reserves	3000–3299	3999
Sales	4000–4299	4399
Purchases	5000–5299	5999
Direct Expenses	6000–6299	6999
Overheads	7000–8299	9997

ALERT: The Bank accounts (1200–1209) and VAT liability (2200–2209) categories float between the assets and liabilities type depending upon whether they hold credit or debit balances.

HOT TIP: If none of the ready-made charts of accounts is close enough to your needs, you can create your own from scratch. It will take a bit of time, but you should have to do it only once.
1. At the Chart of Accounts window, click Add to start and enter a name at the prompt.
2. When the Edit Chart of Accounts dialogue box opens, the category types will be in place already but they will all be empty.
3. Create your categories, with suitable ranges, for each type.

A default chart is created when the software is installed (see page 33). You can add new categories or alter the ranges as needed.

1 In the Company module, click the COA button.

2 Select a Layout – there may be only one – and click Edit.

3 Click on a category to display its subranges.

To adjust a range:

4 Type the new High code for the category or account, or click on the down arrow and select the new highest account (if it has been created).

To add a category:

5 Type a suitable name.

6 Type the Low and High codes, or select them from the lists.

7 Click Save.

8 Close the Edit panel to return to the Chart of Accounts panel, and click Close to end.

ALERT: The Edit Chart of Accounts dialogue box does not give you a clear overview of the whole chart and this can lead to errors. After making any changes, always click Check to get the system to check for overlapping ranges and other errors. You may find it useful to print the chart – click Print to get a hard copy.

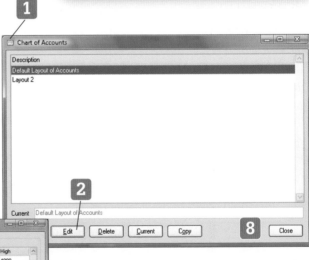

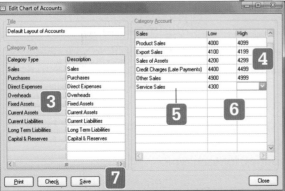

HOT TIP: You can set up a new category before you create the accounts that will go in it, or create the accounts first. The chart is simply a way of grouping the accounts for analysis and is not part of the structure.

Edit the Nominal accounts

You can delete or rename Nominal accounts or create new ones as needed to suit your business. The accounts most likely to need some attention are:

- Stock accounts (numbered from 1000), Sales (4000 onwards) and Purchases (5000 onwards) – these may well need renaming to suit your types of goods or services.

- Overheads (7000 onwards) – these should be checked to see that they agree with your categories of expenses.

1 Switch to the Company module to display the nominal accounts list.

2 Click on the account(s) you want to rename.

3 Double-click on the account or right-click on it and select Edit Record from the pop-up menu.

4 At the record window, edit the Name as required.

5 Save the new name.

6 The panel will be cleared ready for work on another account. Click Next to edit the next selected record or pick one from the N/C drop-down list.

7 Click Close to close the record window and return to the main display.

8 Click on the record(s) again, or click Clear to deselect.

 HOT TIP: You may want to handle computer hardware separately from other office equipment (N/C 0030), as it can be written off in two years, rather than the standard 25 per cent p.a. You will need two accounts, which you might name 'Computer Hardware' and 'Computer Depreciation'.

 ALERT: An account can be deleted very easily – just select it and click Delete – so take extra care.

Do not delete an account unless you are quite sure that you do not need it. An empty account takes up a tiny amount of disk space. And before you start to delete, click the Clear button so that no out-of-sight accounts are selected.

Create an account

When creating an account, remember it must go within the range of the appropriate type – or just outside if the range can be extended to include it. If there is an appropriate category with an unused Nominal code, that is the ideal location for a new account.

1 Click New to start the Nominal Record Wizard.

2 At the opening stage, click Next to get started.

3 Type a Name for the account, then select a Type from the list. Click Next.

4 Select a Category (from the Chart of Accounts). The next available Nominal Code in that category will be allocated to the account. If you do not want the allocated Ref number, change it – but be sure it is in the right range. Click Next.

5 You will be asked whether you want to enter an opening balance. Select Yes if you do, then click Next.

6 Enter the Date and Amount, and check that the default Debit/Credit selection is appropriate. (See the next section for more on opening balances.) Click Next.

7 At the final stage, click Finish to create the new record.

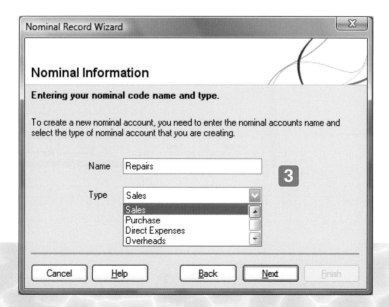

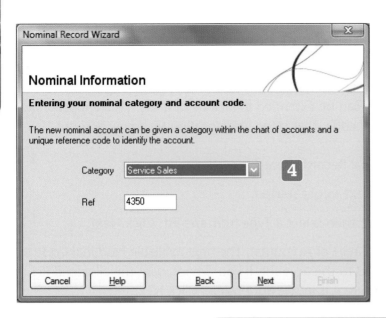

Nominal Record Wizard

Nominal Information

Entering your nominal category and account code.

The new nominal account can be given a category within the chart of accounts and a unique reference code to identify the account.

Category   Service Sales

4

Ref   4350

| Cancel | Help | Back | Next | Finish |

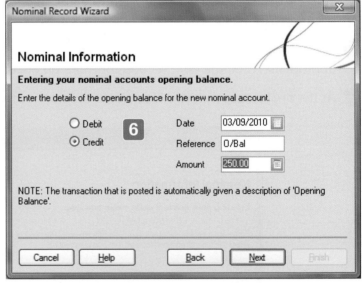

Nominal Record Wizard

Nominal Information

Entering your nominal accounts opening balance.

Enter the details of the opening balance for the new nominal account.

○ Debit   **6**   Date   03/09/2010

⊙ Credit   Reference   O/Bal

              Amount   250.00

NOTE: The transaction that is posted is automatically given a description of 'Opening Balance'.

| Cancel | Help | Back | Next | Finish |

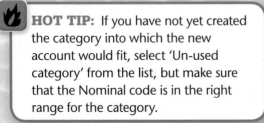

HOT TIP: If you have not yet created the category into which the new account would fit, select 'Un-used category' from the list, but make sure that the Nominal code is in the right range for the category.

ALERT: If you create accounts you may need to adjust the ranges or set up new categories. This can be done before or after creating the accounts.

6 Double-entry book-keeping

Introduction

With day-to-day transactions – sales, purchases and payments – you need to record the details of each transaction only once. When you are recording receipt of a payment, for example, you simply tell the system which account the money is going into, which customer has paid which invoice and how much has been received. The system then handles the double-entry book-keeping for you.

With some transactions you have to make the double entries yourself. The most common examples of these are entering opening balances, and making journal entries and reversals.

Enter an opening balance

Opening balances (O/B) should normally be entered on all accounts where transactions have taken place. In an ongoing business this will probably mean all used accounts, except those of suppliers and customers where debts have been cleared. If the business is just starting, you will need to enter opening balances in the Capital and Bank accounts, and perhaps those for property and other assets.

This can be done through a record window. The balancing entry will automatically be made in the Suspense account (N/C 9998), which serves as a temporary home for values.

1 In the appropriate module, locate the record(s) to be edited. Double-click or click Record to open the record window.

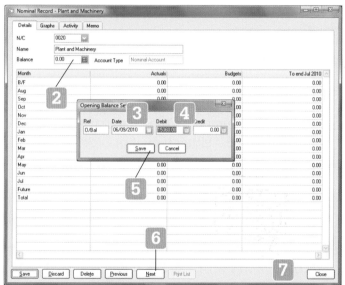

2 Click on the Balance field. The Opening Balance Setup window will open.

3 Set the Date.

4 Enter the value into the Debit or Credit field.

5 Click Save.

6 If several records have been selected, click Next to go to the next one and repeat steps 2 to 5.

7 Click Close to close the record window.

! ALERT: After you have done this, look back at the Nominal accounts display and scroll to the bottom of the list. You should see that the Suspense account contains an amount equivalent (but opposite) to the opening balance(s). This needs to be moved into the appropriate account(s), and to do that we use journal entries.

🔥 HOT TIP: Every opening balance must have an equivalent entry in another account – every debit needs a balancing credit, and vice versa. Remember:

- Debit: movement of value into an account.
- Credit: movement of value out of an account.

For example, when you buy something, it is entered as a debit in the appropriate asset, purchase or expense account and a credit in a bank or supplier's account.

Make a journal entry

A journal entry is a transfer between Nominal accounts. Typical uses include relocating amounts placed in Suspense, and recording depreciation or the revaluation of stock or other assets.

Making a journal entry is one of the few situations where you have to do the double-entry book-keeping yourself rather than leaving it to the system. An entry normally consists of a pair of transactions, one debit, one credit. Sometimes there will be more than two, but the total debits and credits must always balance – you cannot save the entries until they do!

1 Click Journals to open the Nominal Ledger Journals window.

2 Give a Reference to identify the journal.

3 Set the Date.

4 Set the N/C number of the Nominal account into which the value will be moved from Suspense – either type it or pick it from the drop-down list.

5 Type the Details.

6 Enter the amount in the Debit or Credit column – this should be the same side as the original amount which produced the Suspense balancing entry.

7 Repeat steps 4 to 6 for the balancing entry to move the amount out of the Suspense account – this will be the opposite debit/credit to the original.

8 If there are several opening balances to correct, repeat steps 2 to 7 for each of them.

9 Click Save. If the total debit and credit entries are not the same, you will be alerted. You can save and exit from the Journals window only when the entries balance.

HOT TIP: Before you start, make a note of the details of the monies to be moved – the source and target accounts, date, reference and amount.

View records in the Activity display

You can best view the transactions in the Nominal accounts using the Activity display. The same information is shown as in the Activity tab of the Record panel, but you can move more easily between different records here. You can look at the transactions in a preselected set of accounts, and/or select individual accounts once you are in the Activity display window.

1 If you want to look at specific records, select them first.

2 Click Activity.

3 Limit the display, if required, by setting a month, quarter or other period from the Show list.

4 At the Activity window, select a transaction to see its components (if any) in the lower pane.

5 Move through the preselected accounts using the Previous and Next buttons. Or …

6 Select an account from the drop-down list.

7 Click Close when you have finished.

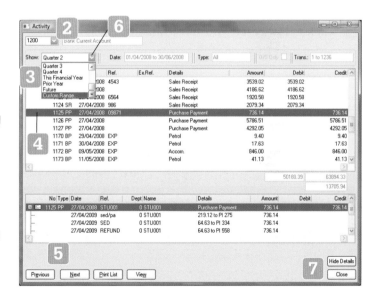

SEE ALSO: You can limit the type and/or date and/or transaction numbers to filter the display so that you can locate records more easily. See Set a Custom Range on the next page.

HOT TIP: The Activity tab of the Nominal Record window shows exactly the same information. However, if you want to view the activity in several accounts, each time you switch to a new account the display reverts to the Details tab and you have to bring the Activity tab back to the front.

Set a Custom Range

An account may have hundreds or thousands of transactions so that it is hard to spot any given one in the full display. This is where the Custom Range facility is valuable.

1 Display the Activity window for an account.

2 Drop down the Show list and select Custom Range.

3 Enter the From and To transaction numbers. And/or ...

4 Select the Transaction Type. And/or ...

5 Set the Date Range.

6 Click OK to apply the settings.

7 Locate the transaction in the filtered display.

8 Click Close when you have finished.

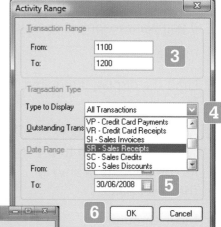

ALERT: The same Custom Range will be applied to all future Activity displays, until you redefine it.

Use the Nominal reports

The Nominal module has nearly 20 ready-made reports, grouped into eight sets:

- Day Books: lists journal entries and reversals.

- Departmental: analyses nominal accounts by departments.

- My Nominal Reports: lists any that you create yourself, either from scratch or by adapting existing reports.

- Nominal Activity: shows the transactions in each Nominal account – with or without inactive accounts.

- Nominal Balances: lists the balance in each account.

- Nominal Budgets: lists the budget reports for the year, half-year or quarter.

- Nominal Details: lists the Nominal accounts, with or without monthly values. Two of these are in CSV (Comma Separated Values) format, which can be read by most databases and spreadsheets. Use it if you want to process the data further using one of these applications.

- Nominal Quick Ratio: lists the assets and liabilities accounts and shows the credit/ debit balance.

Most reports can list all the accounts or those in a selected range. Depending upon the type of report, this can be based on the Nominal code, date, transaction number or department.

1. Click Reports to open the Report Browser.

2. Select a set in the left-hand pane, then select a layout.

3. Choose the output from the toolbar – Preview, Print, File or Email.

4 In the Criteria dialogue box, you can specify a range of Nominal codes, transaction dates or numbers.

5 To use a preset date range, click the pencil icon to the right of the Date fields and select a range.

6 Select a number to preview – half a dozen is often enough.

7 Click OK to generate the report.

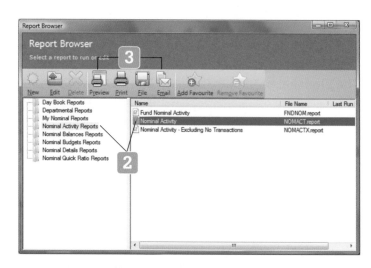

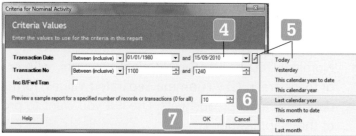

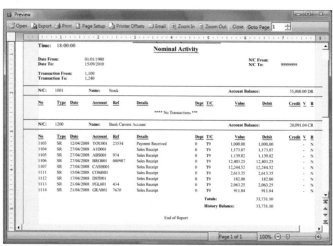

HOT TIP: Always preview before printing any report. It takes only a few moments to check that the report will give you the information that you need and it can save a lot of wasted paper and toner.

7 Working in the
Bank module

Introduction

This module gives you more ways of working with and different ways of looking at those Nominal accounts which are used for the payment and receipt of money. The routines here can be used to make and record payments to suppliers, record receipts from customers, set up recurring payments, move money between accounts, reconcile your records with the bank statements, print cheques, and perform other money-management activities.

Explore the Bank tasks

There are 15 different operations that can be started from the Bank module. All of these can be run from the entries in the Tasks or Links lists and almost all from toolbar buttons. The only 'missing' buttons are for New Recurring Transaction (which can be run from within the Recurring List) and the Cash Register and Deposit Cash routines (which will not be relevant to many businesses). The names may vary slightly, but the routines are the same.

1 Click the Bank bar to open the Bank module.

2 Click Print List if you want a simple list of the accounts and their current balances.

3 Click on a toolbar button if you are not sure where it leads – whichever window it opens can be closed again without doing anything.

ALERT: This window has so many toolbar buttons that they may well not all be displayed on your screen. If there is a double chevron at the right end of the toolbar, click this to reach the overflow.

E Payments and E Reconcile will be present only if electronic banking is enabled.

HOT TIP: Note that in the Bank List, you can select only one account at a time – and for some operations, you don't need to select any.

View a Bank account

The records in the Bank module contain details of each account, as well as recording the transactions that have passed through it. The contact information for the bank can be edited here, if necessary. The Activity tab lists the transactions, with drill-down details where appropriate, e.g. where a single sales receipt covers the payment of several invoices.

1 Select an account.

2 Click Record.

3 Go to the Bank Details and Contact tabs to see or update the details of the bank or your contact within it.

4 Go to the Activity tab to examine transactions that have passed through that account.

5 Click Hide Details if you are not interested in the details of the transactions and want more room for the main display. The button will change to Show Details.

6 Drop down the Show list if you want to view only certain transactions. You can limit the display to a given month, or the reconciled or unreconciled ones, or define a Custom Range.

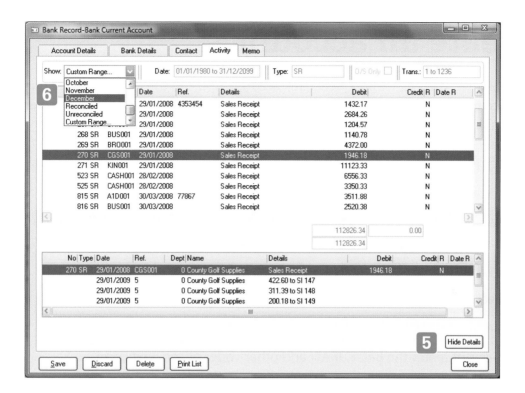

 ALERT: The initial date range is from 01/01/1980 to 31/12/2099! Clearly your records won't cover that range, and it is a fiddly job resetting the calendar to more realistic limits.

 HOT TIP: The Bank accounts can also be opened through the Nominal module, and you must use this to reach the graphs and the budgeting facilities.

 SEE ALSO: The Custom Range is defined here in the same way as it is with other Nominal accounts. See Set a Custom Range on page 92.

Create an account

There are two ways to set up a new bank account. You can use a wizard to set one up from scratch, or use the Duplicate routine if the new account shares details with an existing one. Here's how to use the wizard.

1 Click New on the toolbar to open the wizard, then Next to get past the initial page.

2 Type a name for the account.

3 The wizard will suggest a Ref (Nominal Code) number – you can change this if you like.

4 Click Next.

5 Select the account type – Cheque, Cash or Credit card – and click Next.

6 Enter the first set of bank details (see below for explanations if needed).

7 If relevant, enter the BACS, IBAN and other codes at the next page.

8 Enter the bank's name and address.

9 Enter the name and details of your contact at the bank (if there is a specific person).

10 You can enter an opening balance (if any) as a set of transactions or as a single value. Select and click Next.

11 If you are entering an opening balance, give the date and amount and select either Money in account or Overdrawn.

12 Click Finish to end.

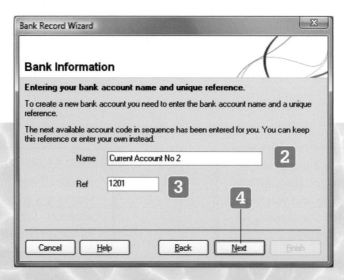

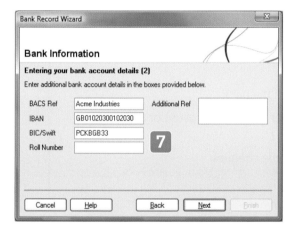

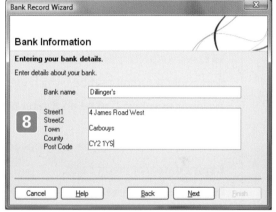

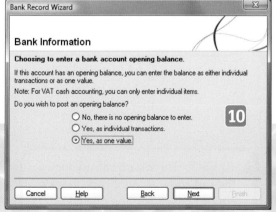

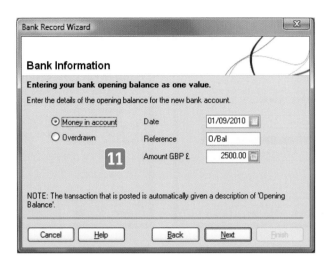

WHAT DOES THIS MEAN?

Sort code: A 6-digit number which identifies the bank.

Account number: Can be an 8-digit number for a bank account or a 16-digit number for a credit card.

Account name: Should be as it appears on the cheques.

Expiry date: For credit cards.

Minimum: The agreed credit or overdraft limit.

BACS: The reference number for BACS (online bank-to-bank) payments.

IBAN: The International Bank Account number, needed only for international transfers.

BIC/Swift: Needed only for international transfers.

Roll numbers: Used by some building societies in addition to account numbers.

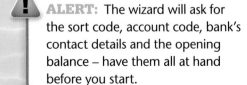

ALERT: The wizard will ask for the sort code, account code, bank's contact details and the opening balance – have them all at hand before you start.

HOT TIP: If the new account is with the same bank as an existing one, select that account and click the Duplicate button. That will copy the details for you. Then you just need to edit the account name, number and opening balance.

Reconcile your accounts

Reconciliation is one of those chores that cannot be automated fully, but at least the Sage 50 system makes it straightforward. As you mark items that match entries in your bank statement, the system calculates and displays the difference between your recorded end balance and that of the bank statement. If they do not match after you have worked through the list, you can see how much it is adrift and will probably have a clear idea of the source of the problem.

1 Select an account.

2 Click Reconcile on the Bank Accounts toolbar.

3 At the Statement Summary dialogue box, enter the Ending Balance from your bank statement – the balance in your Sage 50 Bank account will have been written in as the default.

4 If the statement shows interest earned or bank charges, enter the amounts and select the appropriate N/C codes.

5 Click OK to open the Bank Reconciliation window.

6 Work through the list. Select an unmatched item in the top list. If you can match it with the bank statement, mark it off on the statement and click Match to move it to the Matched list below.

7 If you do not have the time or the information to complete the reconciliation, you can click Save to save the work done so far, then restart the process later using the saved data.

8 When all the items have been reconciled, if the Difference is not 0.00, you need to track down the missing transactions, or identify the ones entered incorrectly. When you have found them, click Adjust and enter the details.

9 When you have finished, click Reconcile.

10 If there is a difference between your Bank account and the statement amount, you can add an adjustment at this point, or choose to ignore the difference.

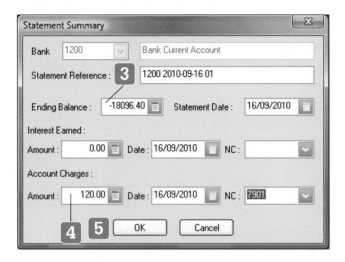

🔥 **HOT TIP:** You can select multiple records and match them in one operation.

Record payments and receipts

There are four routines here. New Payments and New Receipts are designed to handle cash transactions – these can be done in batches if required. The Pay Supplier and Receive Payment are there to record settlement of credit transactions. (These can also be accessed through the Customers and Suppliers modules.)

1 Select a Bank account.

2 Click Payment or select the New Payment task.

3 Set the Date and give a Ref code if required.

4 Select the N/C code of the account for the goods or service.

5 Enter the Details of the sale or purchase.

6 Enter the amount into the Net box – if this is VAT-inclusive, click Calc. Net to split it into Net and VAT.

7 Repeat for any other items.

8 Click Save and then Close.

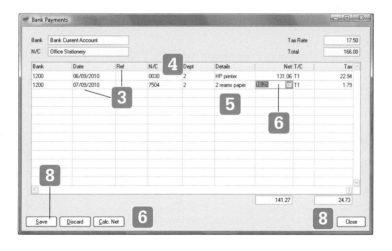

? DID YOU KNOW?

The example here is from the New Payments routine, but the same method is used to process cash receipts.

🔥 HOT TIP: The Accountant Plus and Professional versions of the software have cheque-printing facilities in their payment routines.

Receive payments

Use Receive Payment for recording monies received from credit customers, one at a time. The Receive Payment window shows the outstanding invoices for the selected customer. Receipts can be either allocated to specific invoices or automatically set against invoices in reference number (not date) order.

1 Select the bank account to take the money.

2 Click Customer or select the Receive Payment task.

3 Select the customer from the A/C list.

4 Set the Date and enter the Ref.

5 Enter the Amount of the payment.

6 Click Automatic to set this against invoices. The monies will be allocated from the top down until the amount is exhausted, paying each in full, and the last one whatever is left. Or …

7 Select an invoice and enter an amount or click Pay in Full. If there is a discount, enter this in the end column. Repeat as required.

8 Click Save.

9 Go back to step 3 for the next customer, or click Close.

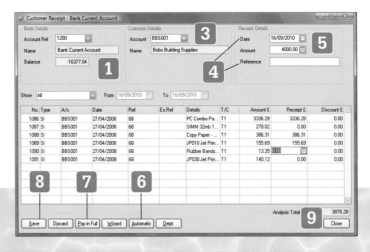

 HOT TIP: Check out the Customer Receipts wizard. You or your accounts staff may find this a simpler way of handling payments and credit notes, as it guides you clearly through the processes.

Pay suppliers

The Receive Payment and Pay Supplier routines are virtually identical in the way that they work, though they look a little different as the Pay Supplier window has a cheque display at the top.

As you enter amounts against invoices, the system calculates the total and shows it in words and figures in the 'cheque' at the top.

1 Select the account from which the payment will be made.

2 Click Supplier.

3 Set the Date and enter the Cheque No. or leave this at BACS.

4 Select the supplier from the Payee drop-down list.

5 Enter the amount on the cheque and click Automatic to allocate this to invoices. Or …

6 Select an invoice and enter an amount or click Pay in Full. This will be added to the total amount in the cheque display at the top. Or …

7 If there is a discount, enter the full Payment, then the Discount – it will be deducted from the payment.

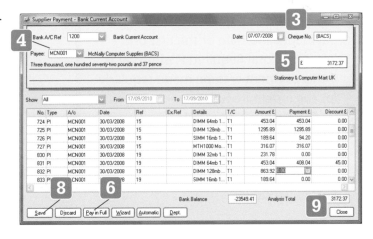

8 Click Save.

9 Go back to step 3 for the next payment, or click Close.

> **! ALERT:** In the Accountant Plus and Professional versions, if a cheque is required, the details will be added to the cheque list for printing later. With the standard Accountant software, the cheque layout in the Payment window is just a convenient way to display the details.

Add a recurring entry

Direct debits, standing orders and other regular payments to suppliers or from customers can be set up as recurring entries and processed automatically. There are two ways to view recurring entries and three ways to start adding a new one. They all do the same job!

1 Click the New Recurring Transaction task in the Bank module to open the Add/Edit Recurring Entry window.

2 Select the Bank account.

3 Select the Transaction Type (see the box below).

4 Select the Nominal Code that the payment is made from and to.

5 Enter the Details to identify the transaction.

6 Set the frequency, number of payments and date of the first one – leave the Total Required Postings at 0 if this payment is to be made regularly for the indefinite future.

7 Enter the Net Amount and the tax if appropriate.

8 Click OK to return to the Recurring Entries window.

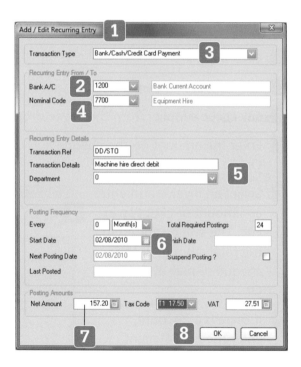

ALERT: Where there is no end date, the entry will be marked 'Perpetual' in the Recurring Entries window. Don't feel over-committed by this. It's only perpetual as long as you want to pay it!

? DID YOU KNOW?

The type of transaction can be Payment, Receipt, Transfer (between bank accounts), payment on account from a customer or to a supplier, or a journal debit or credit. Remember that every journal entry must have a matching debit or credit entry, and you must create these yourself.

View or post a recurring entry

1 Click the Recurring button in the toolbar to open the Recurring Entries window.

2 To change an entry, select it and click Edit.

3 If the entries are all correct, click Process to start posting the transactions.

4 At the Process Recurring Entries window, set the date up to which you want to show transactions.

5 If required, you can edit the Due Date, Net and Tax fields.

6 When you are happy that the entries are correct, click Post.

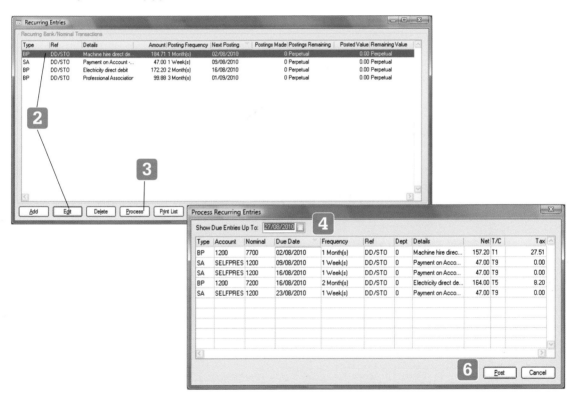

HOT TIP: If you need to know how many times a recurring entry has been paid, select it and click Activity. Among other things, this tells you the number and total of payments to date.

Make transfers

The Transfer routine is used to record the movement of monies between Bank accounts, e.g. restocking petty cash, paying the credit card bill, or transferring cash between your current and deposit accounts at the bank.

1 Click Transfer or select Record Transfer from the Tasks list.

2 Select the account from which to transfer.

3 Select the account to which the money will be transferred.

4 Edit the Description if 'Bank Transfer' does not say enough for you.

5 Enter the Payment Value.

6 Set the Date.

7 Click Save.

8 Repeat from step 2 if there are any more transfers, otherwise click Close.

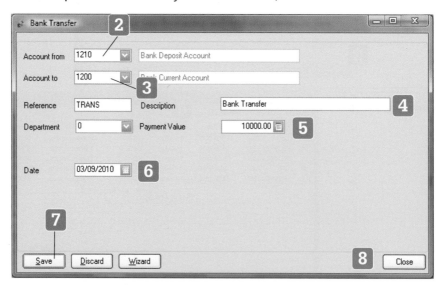

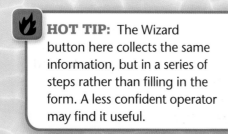

HOT TIP: The Wizard button here collects the same information, but in a series of steps rather than filling in the form. A less confident operator may find it useful.

ALERT: This routine does not actually move the money – you will need to go online to the bank, or arrange the transfer, as well as recording it here.

Produce statements

The Statement button can produce a list of the reconciled transactions, in numerical order and with a running balance, for all those accounts that have seen activity in the current audit trail. You can output statements for selected accounts only.

1 Click the Statement tool.

2 Select the Output mode and click Run.

3 At the Criteria dialogue box, set the range by date if required, then click OK.

4 At the Print dialogue box, set the options as required.

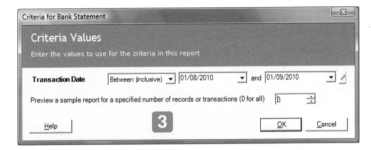

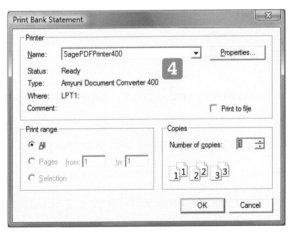

ALERT: The process is kind of backwards – you tell it to run first, then define how to do it! Still, the result is the same.

HOT TIP: Don't use the calendar to set the dates – it takes too long. It's much simpler to type in the start and end dates. Use the format DD/MM/YYYY, e.g. 05/06/2010 is 5 June 2010.

Create reports

The Bank module offers more than 40 summary and detailed reports, reflecting the accounts and transaction routines of the Bank module. The layouts are all fixed, but you control the content by setting the range of dates and reference numbers, and by selecting the Nominal and Bank accounts to include. Most reports can list all the accounts or those in a selected range. Depending upon the type of report, this can be based on the Nominal Code, date, transaction number or department.

1 Click the Reports toolbar button.

2 Select a set, then a layout.

3 Choose the output – Preview, Print, File or Email.

4 In the Criteria dialogue box, you can specify a range of nominal codes, transaction dates or numbers.

5 If you want to check that the criteria select the right things, set a number to preview instead of running the full report.

6 Click OK to generate the report.

What's available

There are 15 sets of ready-made reports:

- Three varieties of Bank payments and receipts: together and separate, detailed and summary.

- Cash payments and cash receipts: detailed and summary.

- Credit card payments and receipts: detailed and summary.

- Customer reports: detailed and summary, in all or just the cash sales.

- Purchase and bank payments: as a single report.

- Reconciled transactions: sorted in different ways.

- Reconciled and unreconciled transactions, and non-reconciled or purely unreconciled.

- Unreconciled transactions: either bank report, payments or receipts.

- Sage Pay reports.

- Sales and Bank receipts: shown together.

- Supplier reports: detailed and summary.

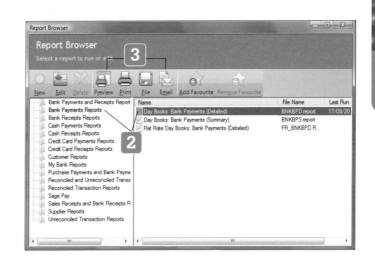

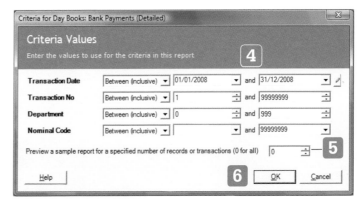

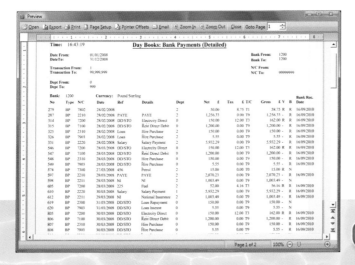

SEE ALSO: You can, of course, create your own reports, or edit any of these, using Report Designer (see Chapter 4).

8 Customers and suppliers

Introduction

In the Sage 50 systems, customers and suppliers are handled in almost identical ways, as you might expect – it is the same trading relationship, but viewed from opposite ends. The examples in this chapter are drawn from the Customers module, but – with rare exceptions – could have come from the Suppliers module.

Create a record

Accounts can be set up from the New button in the customers/suppliers list in those windows that handle invoices, receipts and payments – a blank record opens to take the details. However, the simplest way is to use the New wizard in the Customers and Suppliers modules. This helps to ensure that all essential information is entered and creates an A/C (account) reference for you.

1 Open the Customer module and click New.

2 Click Next to get started and Next after each stage.

3 Enter the name. An A/C Ref will be generated – edit this to make it easier to recognise, if necessary.

4 Enter the address details.

5 Enter the contact details and set the Account Status – normally Open (active, existing client) or New.

6 At the three Additional Information stages, check and adjust the Credit Limit and Terms as required. If terms have been agreed with the customer, tick the checkbox at the second stage – until this is ticked, you will get a reminder every time you open the account.

7 Enter the customer's bank details if payments are to be by BACS.

8 If you are bringing an existing customer onto the system, you may need to set the opening balance. This can be entered as a set of individual transactions, or as a single value.

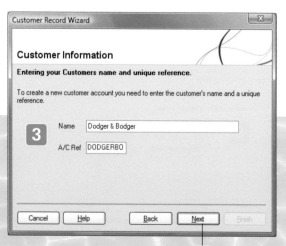

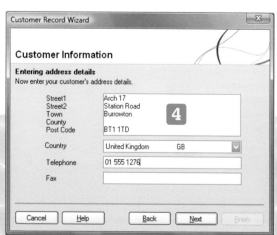

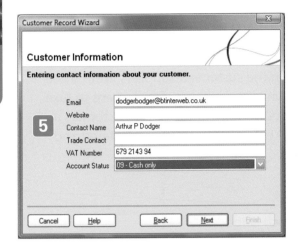

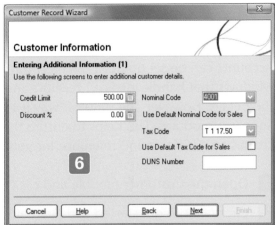

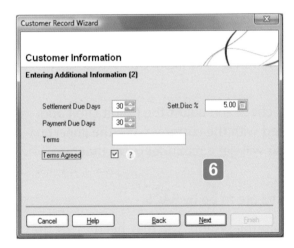

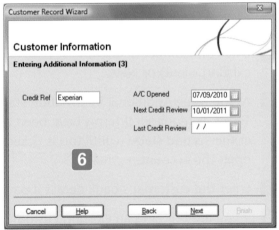

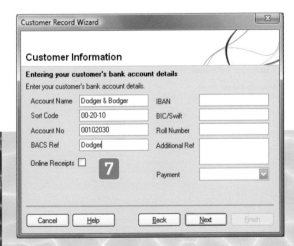

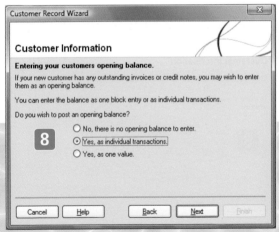

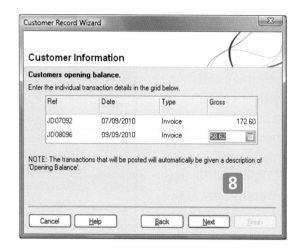

DID YOU KNOW?

If you do not have all the required information about the new customer, or do not have time to fill it in at that point, you can reopen the record and enter the missing details at any time.

HOT TIP: The A/C ref produced by the system is simply the first eight letters in the customer's name – which is fine as long as you don't have several customers starting with the same letters. If the ref clashes with an existing one, you will be offered a variation – typically the last letter will be replaced by '1'.

WHAT DOES THIS MEAN?

Account Status: There to alert you and anyone else in the business of your trading situation with the customer. Initially this would be set to 'New', or 'Open', or 'Cash Only' if you are dubious about them. If you hit problems with them, the status can be changed to 'On Hold' – there is a range of predefined reasons. Additional Status labels can be defined if needed.

View and edit records

The record displays for customers and suppliers show not simply their contact details and terms of trade but also the flow of business to date and the current state of their accounts. You can edit the information on the Details, Defaults, Credit Control and Contacts tabs – supplied through the New Customer Wizard – and also on the Memo tab, where you can add notes as required. The details on the other tabs can be viewed only, not edited.

1 Double-click on the record you want to view or edit, Or ...

2 Select several records and click Record or ...

3 Select the records and click Edit Customer in the Tasks pane.

4 Click on the labels to switch between the tabs.

WHAT DOES THIS MEAN?

The main controls here are in the buttons along the bottom of the window. Some tabs have additional sets of buttons.

Save: Writes any changes into the file.

Discard: Restores the record to how it was before the changes.

Delete: Deletes the whole record, not a transaction. To delete a transaction, use the Corrections routine (see page 54).

Previous: Where several records have been selected, this opens the one above in the list.

Next: Opens the next record in the list.

New Invoice: Opens the Invoicing window (see page 135).

Close: Closes the Record window.

The **Previous** and **Next** buttons are available only if several records were selected before opening the window.

View sales activity

You can view the trading activity with your customers in several different ways. On the Sales tab, you can see a summary of the invoices, credits, balances and receipts for each month, and the details behind each of these figures can be displayed if required.

1 Double-click on a cell to display its details window.

2 Click on the plus sign to the left of the top line to show the details. The plus will become a minus sign.

3 If an item had been paid for, or has had a credit, there will be a plus sign to its left. Click on this to see the credit/payment details.

4 Click on Tidy List to hide the details.

5 Click Close to return to the main display.

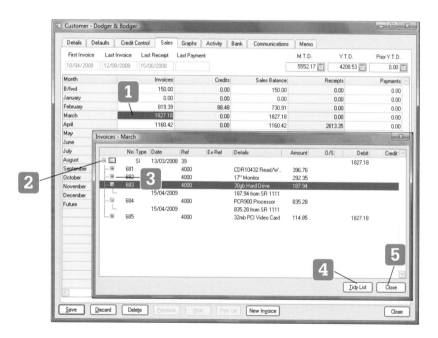

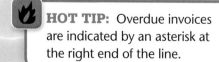

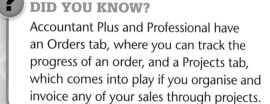

HOT TIP: Overdue invoices are indicated by an asterisk at the right end of the line.

? DID YOU KNOW?

Accountant Plus and Professional have an Orders tab, where you can track the progress of an order, and a Projects tab, which comes into play if you organise and invoice any of your sales through projects.

View the Activity tab

The Activity tab lists all the transactions to date, back to the point when the audit trail was last cleared (see page 185). A busy account can produce a long list of transactions. If you don't want to struggle through the list, use the Show options to restrict the display to a set period, or a custom range of time and/or transaction type.

1 Switch to the Activity tab.

2 Tick the O/S Only box if you want to focus on outstanding items.

3 Select a transaction in the top pane to see its details in the lower pane.

4 Drop down the Show list if you want to see a limited period, or to set a Custom Range.

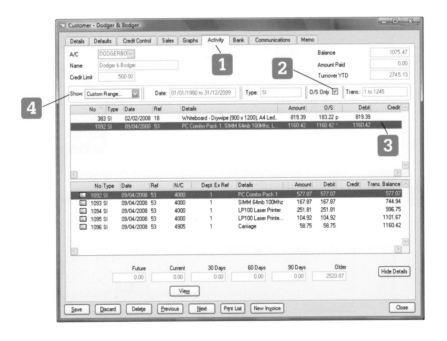

SEE ALSO: The Custom Range is set here as elsewhere. See Set a Custom Range on page 92.

SEE ALSO: We'll come back to the Record window and look at the Credit Control tab in Chapter 10, Credit control.

Use graphs

Graphs can help to show underlying trends that are not immediately visible from the raw data. With the right sort of graph – bar chart, pie chart, line, scatter or Hi-Lo graph – presented in the right way, you can see relationships and changes over time much more clearly than you can by poring over sets of numbers. But beware – you can spend an awful lot of time trying out different display modes and tweaking the layout and design – and not have much to show for it at the end of the day.

1 Switch to the Graphs tab.

2 Click the Options button.

3 Tick to select the data sets – Invoices, Credits and Balances – to include in the graph and click OK.

4 Click the Graph Type button and select a type.

5 Experiment with the tools to see what they do and find settings that you like.

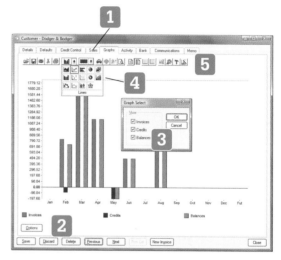

The Toolbar buttons

Working across left to right, the buttons are:

- Open saved graph
- Copy data
- Colours
- Z-clustered series
- Series legend on/off
- Titles
- Properties

- Save as a chart file
- Print
- 3-D
- Zoom
- Vertical grid
- Format titles

- Copy image
- Chart type
- 3D View properties
- X-axis legend on/off
- Horizontal grid
- Tools

? DID YOU KNOW?

The Copy image tool captures the graph as a picture. It can then be pasted into a graphics application, or into a word-processed document as an image.

The Copy data tool copies the figures on which the graph is based. They can then be pasted into a spreadsheet or into a table in a word processor. Just to confuse you, the icon is used for the Cut operation in other Windows applications!

Explore the third dimension!

Sage can display graphs in 3D and – done well – these can add impact to a presentation or report. But they need practice. The basic 3D is easiest to manage – the only setting there is the depth of field. In Full 3D mode, red and blue buttons appear on the model – drag these around the sphere to change the X and Y angle.

1 Switch into 3D mode.

2 Click the 3D View properties button to open the dialogue box.

3 Use the slider to adjust the depth of field.

4 Turn on Full 3D, then ...

5 Drag the buttons around their tracks to adjust the angles.

6 Turn shadows on or off.

7 Click OK when you've finished.

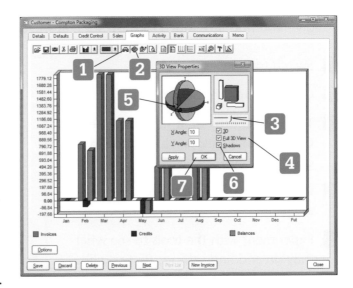

HOT TIP: You can also set the chart options through the Chart properties dialogue box. Click the Properties button to open this.

HOT TIP: If you want to use the graphs productively, take the time to play with the settings until you are happy with them – then leave them alone. These settings will become the defaults for all future graphs.

Search for records

If you have only a few customers and suppliers, it's simple enough to run through the list selecting them individually when you want to examine or process them. Once you get beyond a few, it's worth learning how to use the Search routine. With this, you can pick out those accounts where the values in a field match a given value. For example:

- the customers in a town

- the suppliers whose invoices are due

- trading partners where the annual turnover is above £10,000 or those below £500.

The example here is from the Customer module, but the Search routine is used in the same way in all modules.

1 Click Search.

2 In the Join column, select Where.

3 Click into the Field column and select a field from the list.

4 Click into the Condition column and select how the field and value are to relate.

5 Type the Value.

6 Click Apply. The customer list will now display only those records that match the criteria.

7 If the simple search has done the job, click Close. If not, try a more complex search – read on.

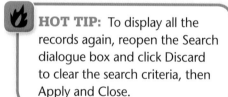

HOT TIP: To display all the records again, reopen the Search dialogue box and click Discard to clear the search criteria, then Apply and Close.

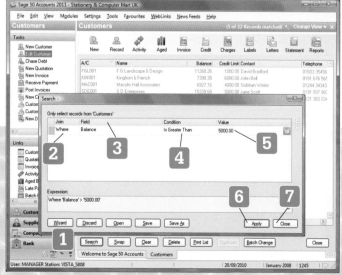

Multiple field searches

Conditions can be set on as many fields as necessary, to select very specific sets of records. The conditions can be joined in two ways:

- Use And if both conditions must apply.
- Use Or where records are selected if either or both conditions apply.

1 Start the search as normal and set up the first condition.

2 Click into the Join box of the next line and select And or Or.

3 Define the second condition.

4 Click Apply.

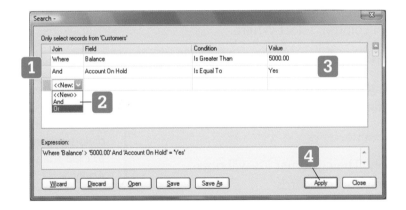

? DID YOU KNOW?

You can set as many conditions, linked by Ands and Ors, as you need. If the search doesn't do the job, click Discard, then Apply to restore the full display of records, before trying a new search.

🔥 HOT TIP: You can set up the search through a wizard. The results are exactly the same – it just walks you through the steps given above. Click Search to open the dialogue box, then click Wizard to start.

Produce customer reports

There are 12 sets of ready-made reports that can be obtained from the Customer module.

- The Customer Details and Sales Contacts reports are useful practical summaries, while the Top Customer reports highlight the ones to look after.

- The Customer Activity, Daily Transaction, Day Book, Departmental and EC Sales reports provide a range of ways to view and analyse your trading patterns.

We'll come back to the Customer Invoice reports when we look at invoicing in Chapter 9, and the Aged Debtor and Credit Control reports in Chapter 10.

To produce a report:

1. Click Reports to open the Report Browser.

2. Select a set in the left-hand pane, then select a layout.

3. Choose the output: Preview, Print, File or Email.

4. In the Criteria dialogue box, you can define a range of accounts. You may also be able to set a range of dates, transaction numbers and/or Nominal Codes, depending upon the report.

5. If you are outputting to a printer, set a number to preview a sample.

6. Click OK to generate the report.

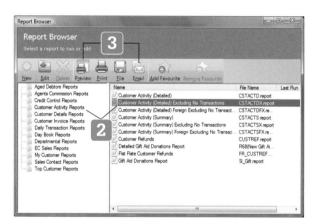

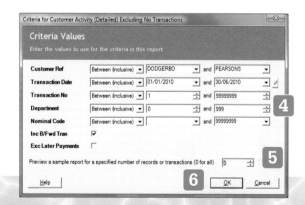

ALERT: If you want to send the statements to all customers or to a continuous set from the customer list, do not select any at this stage.

Produce statements

The Customers and Suppliers modules also have a selection of ready-made labels, letters and statements, some designed for output onto plain paper, others onto Sage stationery. Here's how statements can be produced:

1 Select the customer(s) to whom you want to send the statements.

2 Click Statement.

3 Select the layout. Note that there are different sizes of paper as well as styles of statement.

4 Choose the output: Preview, Print, File or Email.

5 At the Criteria dialogue box, set a range of Transaction Dates if this will be useful, or leave at the defaults to include all current transactions.

6 Set a number to preview if you want to check the outputs.

7 Click OK to generate the report.

8 You will be asked whether you want to update the communication history. If you are sending out statements, this would be a good idea.

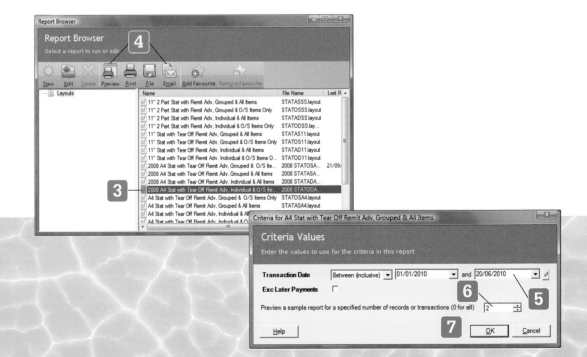

A preview of a report from the Customer module is shown below.

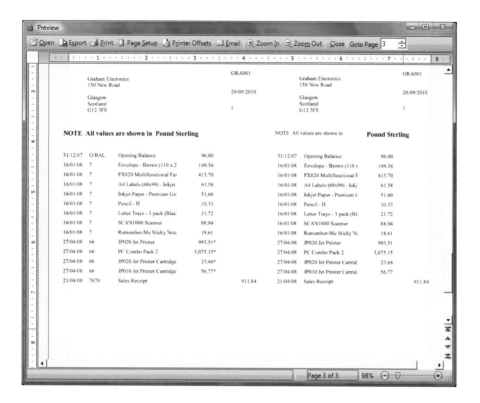

 HOT TIP: Remember that you can use a search to filter the customer list – that may be much simpler than working through selecting them individually.

 SEE ALSO: As with other reports, if there isn't one that meets your requirements, you can edit an existing one, or create a statement from scratch (see Chapter 4).

 ALERT: You must select at least one customer before clicking the Statement button – this routine does not assume you want them for all customers if you select none.

Print labels

Labels are produced in the same way as other reports, but you will probably need to edit the report to change the label size. The Report Designer has the specification of a couple of dozen standard labels and if these don't suit, you can easily define your own. Do a test run before you try to print for real.

1 Select enough customers to fill a sheet of labels, then click Labels.

2 The Report Browser window will open. Select a layout.

3 Click Preview to see how it looks. If you're happy with it, print a sheet to check that the layout works, otherwise carry on through the steps.

4 Click Edit to take it into Report Designer.

5 Open the Format menu and select Labels & Forms.

6 At the Label Details dialogue box, select a Preset label size if your labels are listed. Or ...

7 Click the Advanced button and define the label size and layout.

8 After editing, save the design and close Report Designer.

9 Back at the Labels dialogue box, select the output mode and continue as for statements.

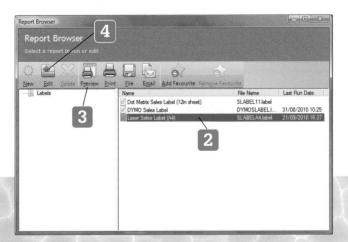

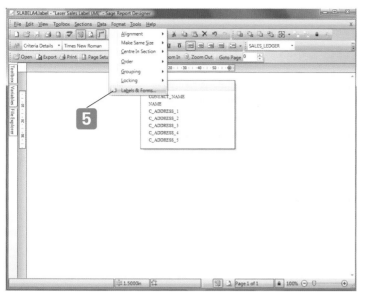

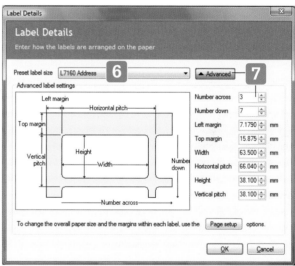

🔥 HOT TIP: If the measurements are in inches and you would prefer metric, close the Label Details dialogue box, then select Options from the Tools menu. At the Options dialogue box you can change the measurement system.

9 Invoices

Introduction

There are different invoice structures for products and services. When creating a Product invoice, on each item line you select a product from your stock list and enter how many. The system then fills in the details, unit price and total cost for you. With a Service invoice you have to type in the details and work out the costs yourself.

When a sale involves both materials and labour, there are two possible solutions:

- Set up labour as a 'Product', with the sales price being the hourly rate. You may need several records for different types of skilled and unskilled labour. The job can then be processed through a Product invoice.

- Include materials in the details of a Service invoice. The catches with this are that you will have to calculate material costs and that product elements will not be posted automatically to the relevant Nominal accounts.

Explore the Invoicing window

New invoices can be produced directly from the Customer module, but it's probably better to work from the Invoicing window. Here, as well as creating invoices you can edit existing ones and create credit notes or pro formas.

1 Click Invoice List in the Links pane to open the Invoicing window.

2 To view or edit an invoice, double-click on it. Or ...

3 Select the invoice(s) and click the New/Edit button on the toolbar.

4 If the invoice has not yet been posted, you can edit it.

5 Click Save to save any changes. Or ...

6 Click Discard to ignore the edits and go back to the original version.

7 If several items were selected in the Invoicing window, use Previous and Next to navigate between them

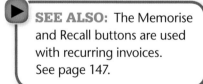

SEE ALSO: The Memorise and Recall buttons are used with recurring invoices. See page 147.

WHAT DOES THIS MEAN?

Credit note: Issued where a customer has been invoiced for goods or services that for some reason were not supplied or have been returned.

Pro forma invoice: Sent if you require the customer to pay in advance for the goods or service. When payment is received, it should be converted to a normal invoice.

Create a Product invoice

The basic design of an invoice is the same whether it is for a product or a service. There is always the following:

- Invoice No. – generated automatically.

- Date – also set for you, but can be changed if necessary.

- A/C Ref – selecting this pulls the name and address into the heading area on the top left.

- Order No. – if the customer has given one.

- VAT and the Totals – calculated by the system.

In a Product invoice you also need to specify the items and the quantity of each.

1 Click Clear if any invoices are selected.

2 Click the New/Edit button in the toolbar.

3 If Product is not the default format, select it.

4 Set the date.

5 Enter an invoice no. if required, or allow the system to generate one automatically.

6 Select the A/C code from the list. The customer's details will be copied into the address block in the top left.

7 For a defined product, select its code from the drop-down list; its description and price will be written in for you. If it is not in the list, click New and add it to your stock list now.

8 Enter the quantity. The Net will then be calculated.

9 If you want to edit the description, add a comment or change the price or other aspect, click the arrow icon by the Description field to open the Edit Item Line dialogue box.

10 Edit or add details as required – to give a discount, enter either the percentage or the actual amount. Click OK when you've finished to return to the Invoice window.

11 Repeat steps 7 to 9 for each item. If the running total triggers a new discount level, you will be alerted.

12 Click Save.

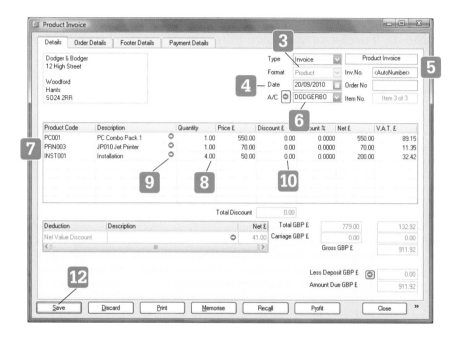

Change the details of a product

You can edit the description of a product or add further details through the Edit Item Line window. The quantity, price, discount and other values can also be entered or edited here rather than on the invoice, if you prefer.

1 At the Invoice window, click on the fat arrow at the end of the Description field of the item you want to edit.

2 The Edit Item Line window will open.

3 Edit the Description if required. This will be shown on the invoice.

4 Add comments, if useful for your own purposes. These will be visible only in the invoice's record on your system.

5 Edit the quantity, price or other values if required.

6 Click OK to close the window and return to the invoice.

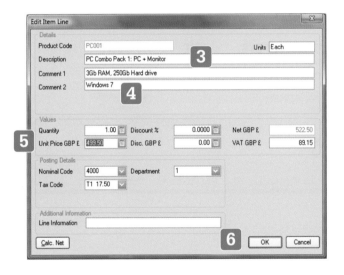

 ALERT: Note the Calc. Net button at the bottom. If the unit price is VAT-inclusive, click this to calculate the net price and the VAT.

SEE ALSO: Creating an invoice or credit note does just that and no more. They are not posted onto the system until you run through the update routine, and they will need to be printed and sent out to the customer. See pages 143 (Print an invoice) and 145 (Update ledgers).

Further details

Many invoices can be completed simply using the top panel. The other panels allow you to add or adjust the details.

- Use the Order Details panel to change the delivery address or contact details from the defaults, or to add any notes.

- Use the Footer Details panel to add a carriage charge, or to alter the default charge, or to adjust discounts and terms.

- If a payment has been received, this can be recorded on the Payment Details tab. The money can be allocated to that invoice, or as a general payment to the account.

1 Switch to the Order Details panel.

2 The Customer Order No. and Order Taken By fields will probably need attention.

3 Check other details and change as necessary.

4 Switch to the Footer Details panel.

5 Enter the Carriage details – costs, codes and courier if different from the defaults.

6 Adjust the terms as needed.

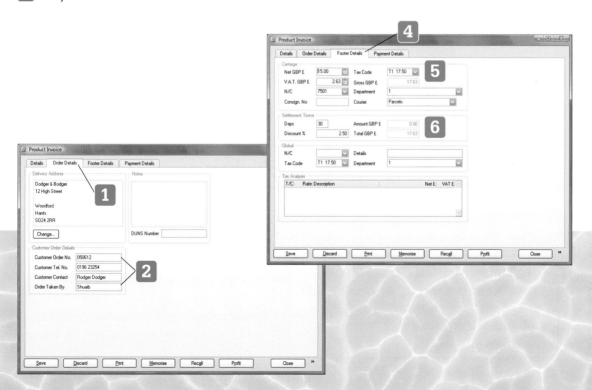

7 Switch to the Payment Details panel.

8 Enter the Ref and Amount.

9 Set the Payment Type, posting it against the account or the invoice.

10 Click Save.

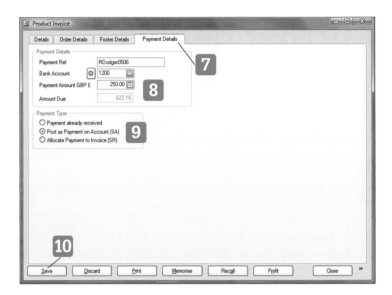

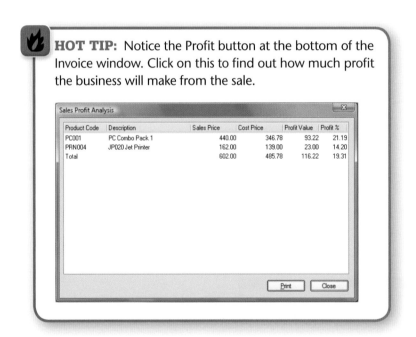

HOT TIP: Notice the Profit button at the bottom of the Invoice window. Click on this to find out how much profit the business will make from the sale.

HOT TIP: If you use couriers who offer parcel tracking through their websites, add their names and site details to the Couriers list – use Settings, Internet Resources to reach this list.

Create a Service invoice

1 Begin as for a Product invoice.

2 Drop down the Format list and select Service.

3 Select the customer from the A/C list.

4 Type the details of the job.

5 Enter the Amount.

6 To add an item, press Tab or click into the next blank line and repeat steps 4 and 5.

7 Change the Order, Footer and Payment Details as necessary.

8 Click Save.

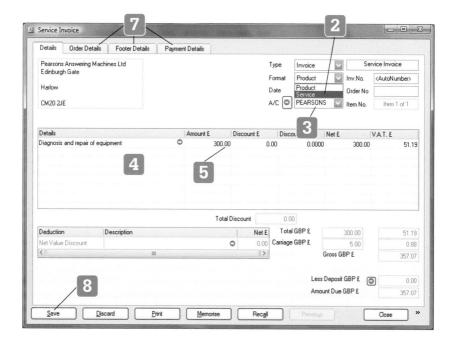

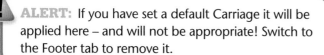

ALERT: If you have set a default Carriage it will be applied here – and will not be appropriate! Switch to the Footer tab to remove it.

Create a credit note

Credit notes are the mirror image of invoices. Probably the most important thing with these is to make sure that the products or services match those on the original invoice. Have prices changed since it was issued? Did you give a discount?

1 Click Invoice List in the Links pane to open the Invoicing window.

2 Click Clear to deselect all invoices in the list.

3 Double-click on the original invoice to open it so you can check its details.

4 Select Credit as the Type. The Format should be Product or Service to match the invoice.

5 Enter the details and price of the credited item or service.

6 Double-click on the Description to open the Edit Item Line window if you need to edit any of the details.

7 Enter any collection or return information on the Order Details tab.

8 Click Save.

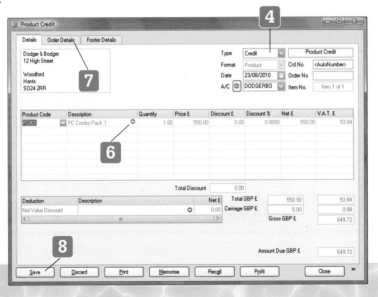

 ALERT: If you are changing the Format from Product to Service, or vice versa, you must do this before starting to enter any of the details.

Print an invoice

Whether you are printing one invoice or many, the steps are the same. The difference is in how you start.

- With a single invoice or credit note, it is simplest to print it while you are creating it. Just click the Print button on the Invoice window. Note that the invoice is automatically saved when you do this.

- If you are processing a set of invoices, it is more efficient to start printing from the Invoicing window.

1 Open the Invoicing window.

2 Select the invoices and click Print.

3 The Report Browser window will open and display the available invoice layouts. Pick one.

4 Select Preview to check the output on screen before printing.

5 If the layout works, you can print from the Preview window, or close it and click Print in the Invoicing window.

6 Close the Report Browser window.

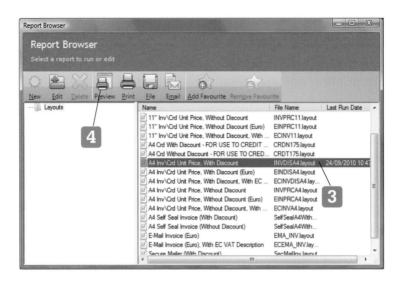

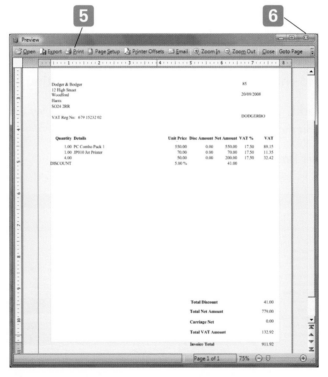

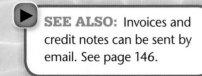

SEE ALSO: Invoices and credit notes can be sent by email. See page 146.

Update ledgers

When you create and save an invoice or credit note, its information is stored in your files, but the effect of the transaction on other accounts is not recorded immediately. To 'post' the data to the relevant customers' and Nominal accounts, you must use the Update button.

The system always shows the transactions it has performed. These can be output to paper or file, if required, or simply viewed on screen.

1 Select the Post Invoices task in the Customers module, if necessary, to open the Invoicing window.

2 If only certain invoices are to be posted, select them first – otherwise all the unposted invoices will be processed.

3 Click Update.

4 If a paper copy is needed, select Printer; if you need a file copy for future reference, select File; otherwise select Preview.

5 Click OK.

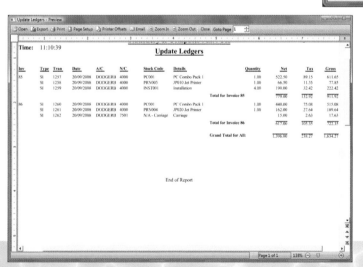

Send invoices by email

If your customers are able and willing to accept invoices by email, it is quicker, simpler and cheaper to send them this way than to print them and send them by post. There are two ways to send an invoice by email: directly from the Invoicing window, or via the Report Browser.

1 Select the invoice(s) in the Invoicing window.

2 Click the Email button in the toolbar.

3 You will probably be asked whether you want to send the report as an attachment. Click Yes.

4 The Provider options are MAPI and SMTP. These are different ways of handling email. Check with your email provider which to use, or do a test email and see whether it goes through. If it doesn't, try the other option.

5 There are nine possible formats. Either PDF or HTML will produce a nicely formatted invoice which the customer can print if they wish.

6 Click OK to send the email.

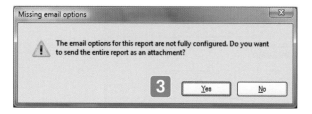

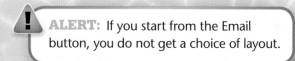

? DID YOU KNOW?

If you start from the Print button, you can choose the layout. If the layout is designed for emailing, all you need to do is click Email to generate it and send it off. With the other layouts, you will go through the Send as Attachment routine shown above.

! ALERT: If you start from the Email button, you do not get a choice of layout.

Create a recurring invoice

If you provide a regular service or supply of goods to a customer, you can set up a recurring invoice so that you do not have to enter the same details every time.

1 Create the (product or service) invoice as normal.

2 Click Memorise to open the Memorise dialogue box.

3 Type a Reference to identify the invoice and add a description.

4 Set the Frequency.

5 Leave the Total Required at 0 if this will be a long-running regular transaction.

6 Set the Start Date.

7 Click Save to return to the Invoice window.

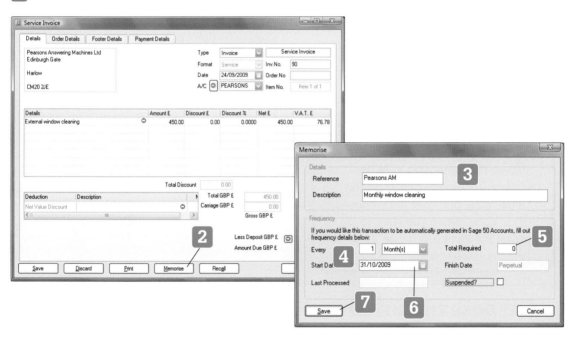

HOT TIP: When you click Save, the invoice data is saved and the window cleared ready for the next one. So, if you click Save before Memorise (easily done!), you will have lost it – temporarily. Open the invoice from the Invoicing window and carry on from where you left off.

Repeat invoices

Recurring invoices are not generated automatically at the required dates. The first of the recurring invoices is generated when it is set up, and would presumably have been posted and printed at that time. When subsequent ones are required, you need to run the Recurring Invoices routine. It's very straightforward.

1 At the Invoicing window, click Recurring to open the Memorised and Recurring Invoices window.

2 Click Process to open the Process Recurring Entries window.

3 Set the date to Show transactions up to.

4 Clear the checkboxes for any entries that you do not want.

5 Click Process to generate the invoices.

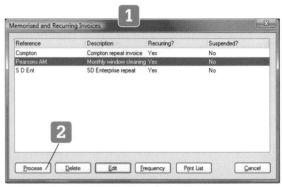

? DID YOU KNOW?

If an invoice is likely to be repeated, but not at regular intervals, it is still worth memorising it. At the Memorise dialogue box, fill in the Details area, but leave the Frequency fields alone. When you want to repeat the invoice in future, click Recall and select it from the list.

WHAT DOES THIS MEAN?

In the Memorised and Recurring Invoices window, there are six buttons along the bottom. We've used Process, and Cancel is obvious. Here's what the rest do:

Delete: Deletes the selected entry from the recurring list. It does not delete any invoices.

Edit: Opens the Invoice window if you want to change any details, price, quantity, etc. on the invoice.

Frequency: Opens a dialogue box where you can change the frequency settings.

Print List: Prints the information shown in this window. It does not give details of dates or frequency of the recurrences.

Process invoices in batches

Invoices and credit notes for your customers are normally dealt with through the Invoicing window, where they can be created, printed and the transactions posted to the ledgers. There are also batch invoices and credits routines in the Customer module, which are there to record the transactions when invoices or credit notes have been produced manually. In the Supplier module, they are the main way to record your transactions.

1 In the Suppliers (or Customers) window, click Invoice.

2 Select the account from the A/C list.

3 Enter the date and your reference.

4 Select the nominal account from the N/C list

5 Enter the Net amount.

6 If the price is VAT-inclusive, click Calc. Net.

7 Repeat steps 2 to 7 as needed.

8 Click Save, then Close.

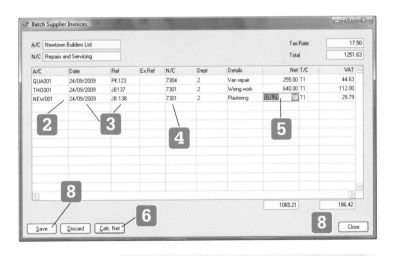

HOT TIP: An invoice can be recorded in a single line. If it is for several items and you want to record each separately, use a new line for each, but keep the same Ref code.

? DID YOU KNOW?

These are handled in almost exactly the same way as invoices. The key point to note is that the reference number here must be that of the invoice against which the credit is being given, so look this up in the customer or supplier's Activity tab before you start.

10 Credit control

Introduction

Good control of your cash flows – in and out of the business – is an essential part of successful management. To keep control of those flows, you need to be able to find out quickly and easily how much money is owing, for how long, and to whom and from whom. Sage 50's credit control facilities can give you that information quickly and easily.

Chase debts

The Chase Debt window is the key place for work on customer credit control. The details listed here are those which you might find useful when chasing debts – how much is overdue, the phone number, contact name, etc. You can filter it to show different categories of debt, and sort it into order on any column, e.g. the amount owing.

1 Go to the Customer module and from the Tasks list, select Chase Debt.

2 In the Include invoices due within the next box, set the number of days ahead to look.

3 In the Show field, select the category of debt, e.g. Outstanding, Overdue, Promised, or by age of debt, to filter the display.

4 Click once on a column header to sort the records into ascending order of that column.

5 Click a second time to sort into descending order.

SEE ALSO: The Chase Debt window has a lot of buttons in its toolbar. Some of these were covered in Chapter 8: Record, Activity, Reports, Letters and Statements.

ALERT: The Chase Debt window is for handling payments from customers. There are equivalent tools and routines for handling payments to suppliers in the Manage Payments window, which you can start from the Suppliers module. We'll come back to these at the end of this chapter.

Use Day Sales Analysis

The analysis window shows you how much is outstanding and overdue. You can see this as a graph, if you want an overview of how the business is doing, or in detail. The graphs give you an overview of the payment patterns. The Details tab lists your customers and their debts to you.

1 Click Analysis to open the Days Sales Analysis window.

2 Switch to the Days Sales Outstanding or Overdue tabs to see the graphs.

3 Use the Details tab to see exactly how much is owing and for how long.

4 Click on the headings to sort by the amount or the age of the debt.

5 Click Print List for a list of customers. This will be in the same order as in the window.

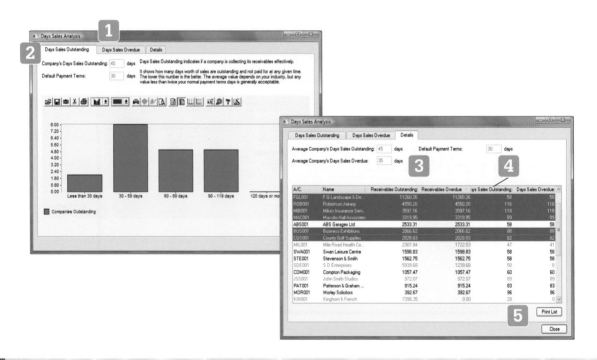

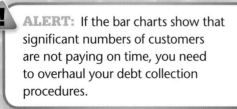 **ALERT:** If the bar charts show that significant numbers of customers are not paying on time, you need to overhaul your debt collection procedures.

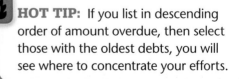 **HOT TIP:** If you list in descending order of amount overdue, then select those with the oldest debts, you will see where to concentrate your efforts.

View the Communications history

Anyone who runs a business dealing mainly with credit customers – especially if it is a smaller business and the customers are larger firms – knows the difficulty of finding the right balance between prompting the slower payers with sufficient vigour to be taken seriously and harassing them to the point where you lose future custom. Life is simpler in those countries which have strict limits on how quickly debts must be paid!

The Communications routine allows you to keep a track on when a customer was contacted and what was agreed.

1 Select the customer.

2 Click Communications to open the customer's record at the Communications tab. This shows any contacts made to date.

3 To see the details of any communication, double-click on the line or select it and click Edit.

4 The details can be edited, if necessary.

5 Click Save if you make any changes.

6 Click Close to return to the Communications window.

 HOT TIP: If a customer is over their credit limit, you will get this warning message whenever you view their record. It's annoying – it's meant to be annoying. To stop it appearing, either get your customer to pay at least some of the debt, or extend their credit limit if they warrant it.

Record a new contact

If you send out reminder and chasing letters using the Sage routines, these can be added to the customer's communication history automatically. Phone calls, or other communications made from outside the Sage system, should also be recorded, but these need to be done by hand. It's simple and quick to do.

1 Select the customer and click Communications to open the Communications tab.

2 Click New to record a new contact.

3 In the Communication Details section, select Telephone, Letter/Fax/Email or Meeting. The details will vary according to the nature of the contact.

4 Fill in the details, and the outcome or results.

5 If the customer promises to pay, record the amount and due date.

6 Click Save to store the details and return to the Communications display.

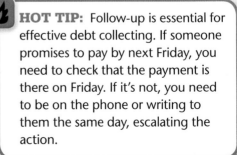

? DID YOU KNOW?

If you want to record the length of your phone calls, start the New contact routine before you make the call. For telephone contacts, there is a Timer display. Click Start when you pick up the phone and Stop when you put it down again, and the duration will be calculated.

HOT TIP: Follow-up is essential for effective debt collecting. If someone promises to pay by next Friday, you need to check that the payment is there on Friday. If it's not, you need to be on the phone or writing to them the same day, escalating the action.

Manage your cash flow

The Cash Flow window shows the state of the bank account(s) if payments are made and received on their forecast dates. When using this, it is important to remember that it is based on guesswork – when figures are shown to the exact penny it is all too easy to think that they are exact.

1 Click the Cash Flow button to open the Cash Flow window.

2 In the Bank Accounts area at the top right, tick the boxes for those accounts that you want to include in the running balance.

3 Click on the calendar icons to change the From and Forecast up to dates.

4 Tick the Inc? checkbox to include the receipt or payment in the running balance – or clear the checkbox if you decide that the money will not come in or go out on or before that day.

5 Scroll down to see the balance over time.

6 Click Graph if you'd like a visual display.

ALERT: When you are deciding which items to include, you may find it simpler to switch to the other tabs where regular and forecast payments and receipts are listed separately.

HOT TIP: The Send To button will export the data to Excel if you want to process it further. Just click and Sage will fire up Excel (assuming it's installed on the computer!) and load into it the data from the Cash Flow window.

The cash flow graph

Graphs tell the story behind numbers. It's much easier to spot high points and low points on a graph than in a column of numbers. Look at the two here. The green bars are receipts, the blue are payments, and the red are the balance in the account at the end of each day. In the top graph, you can see that things are running along nicely – there's a substantial payment at one point, but it is absorbed by the balance. The second graph shows trouble ahead. Those two large payments create an overdraft of nearly £10,000 and although it's soon reduced to around £2,000, action may be needed.

1 Click Graph on the Cash Flow window to display the flows in a graph.

2 Drag the slider, or click the end arrows to scroll through the time.

3 If problem points are spotted, click Cancel to return to the Cash Flow window to see what can be done.

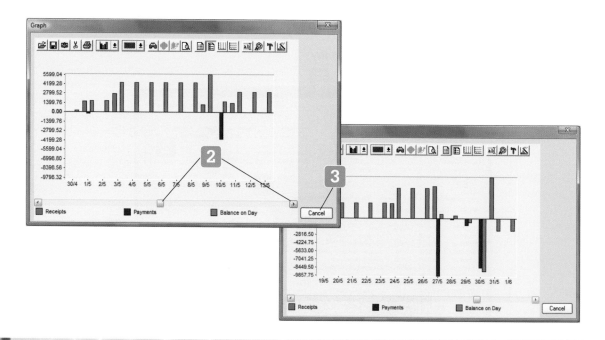

ALERT: There are basically three ways to deal with temporary cash flow crises:
- Delay payments – if they will then be overdue, get the agreement of the suppliers to keep their goodwill.
- Speed up receipts – can older debts be chased more vigorously? Can any advance payments be organised?
- Arrange overdraft facilities – an obvious solution, but can be expensive.

Use Aged Analysis

The Aged Analysis window shows the amounts owing by the customers (or to the suppliers) in each ageing period. This can cover all records, or selected ones. The analysis can also be started from the toolbar button in the Customers and Suppliers windows, and should be done from there if you want to see only select records.

1 To select accounts, go to the Customers or Suppliers window, and select from there.

2 Click Aged.

3 Set the report date and the date to include payments to, and click OK.

The Aged Balances window will open, showing summary information for the selected account(s). Note the totals at the bottom.

4 Switch to the Graph tab to see the totals as a graph.

5 For a closer look at an account, double-click on it (or select it and click Detailed).

6 The Detailed Aged Analysis window lists the invoices. Scroll across to see more details.

7 Click Close to return to the Aged Balances window.

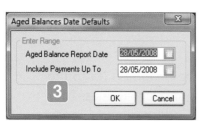

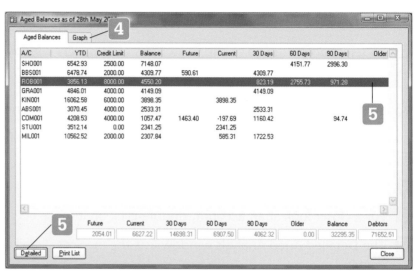

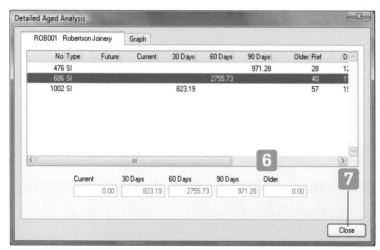

ALERT: In the Aged Balances window, the records are listed in their current order in the Customers/Suppliers window, and this cannot be changed. If you want the records in balance or credit limit order, set this before you click Aged.

HOT TIP: When you run the Aged Analysis from the Chase Debt window, the order in which records are listed – and the selections (if any) – may vary and is not to be relied upon.

Apply credit charges

Charges runs a wizard to apply charges on overdue accounts. To be able to do this, you need to set up finance rates in the Terms tab of the Configuration Editor and turn on Can Charge Credit on your customer records – and, of course, you must agree the terms with your customers!

1 In the Chase Debt or Customer List window, click Charges to start the wizard.

2 At the first step you will be prompted to make a backup before going any further. Do so, unless you have already created one earlier in the day.

3 Set the date up to which charges are to be calculated.

4 All customers with outstanding invoices will be listed. Select those that are to be charged.

5 All of those customers' outstanding invoices will be listed. Select those to include – there may be disputed or other special ones that should not be charged.

6 The wizard now has all it needs. Click Finish to apply the charges.

7 You will be shown the charges which have been applied. Click Print to make a hard copy.

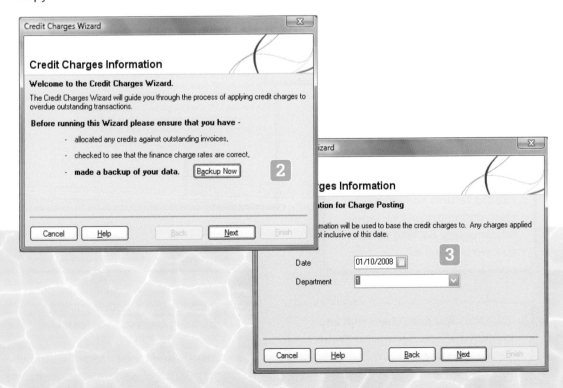

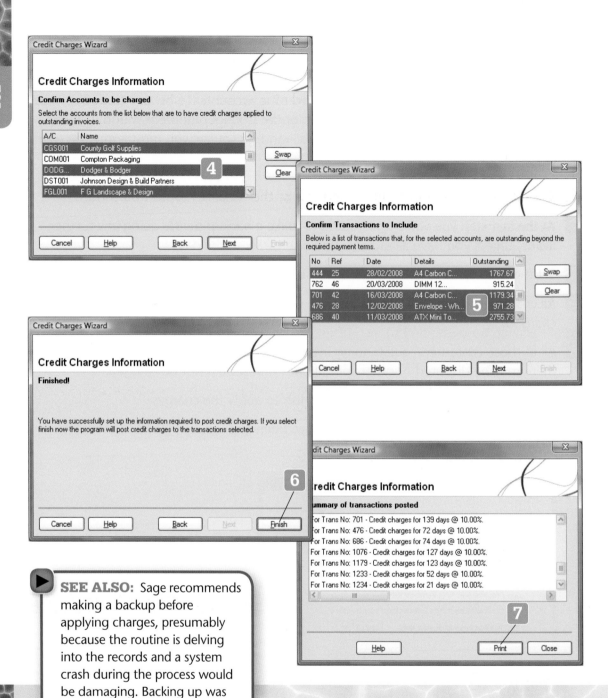

SEE ALSO: Sage recommends making a backup before applying charges, presumably because the routine is delving into the records and a system crash during the process would be damaging. Backing up was covered on page 57.

ALERT: You must check that any credits have been set against invoices before you start.

HOT TIP: As the whole process takes a while, whether you are charging one customer or lots, it's probably best to do this once a month, and for all relevant customers.

Write off a debt

Write-offs, refunds and returns are all handled by a wizard that is started from the Write Off button in the Task list of the Customer module or the Chase Debt window. Here's how a write-off is managed – the other types and refunds and returns are similarly straightforward.

1 Click the Customer Write Off/Refund task or the Write Off toolbar button.

2 At the Write Off, Refunds and Returns Wizard, select Write off Customer Transactions.

3 Click Next.

4 Select the customer. Click Next.

5 Select the transaction(s) to be written off. Click Next.

6 Set the date and add a reference for the operation. Click Next.

7 At the final stage, the details collected by the wizard will be shown. Click Finish to post the write-off.

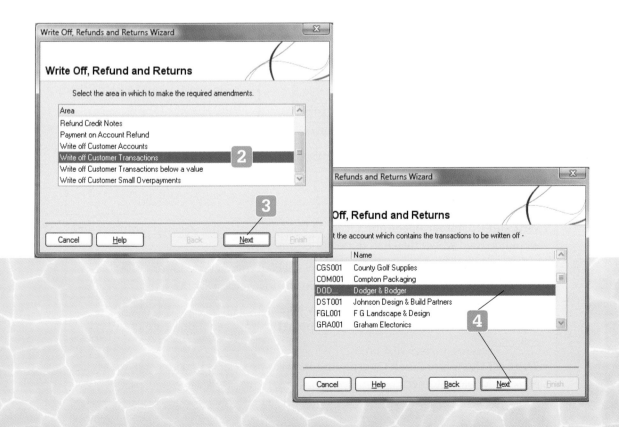

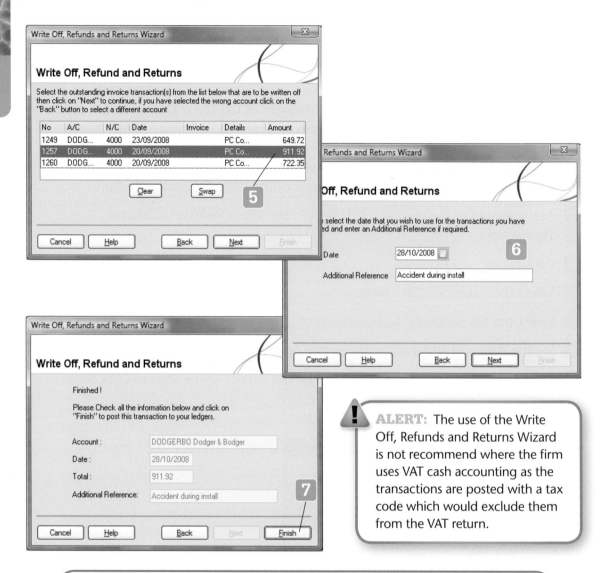

Write Off, Refunds and Returns Wizard

Write Off, Refund and Returns

Select the outstanding invoice transaction(s) from the list below that are to be written off then click on "Next" to continue, if you have selected the wrong account click on the "Back" button to select a different account

No	A/C	N/C	Date	Invoice	Details	Amount
1249	DODG...	4000	23/09/2008		PC Co...	649.72
1257	DODG...	4000	20/09/2008		PC Co...	911.92
1260	DODG...	4000	20/09/2008		PC Co...	722.35

Clear   Swap   **5**

Cancel   Help   Back   Next   Finish

Refunds and Returns Wizard

Off, Refund and Returns

select the date that you wish to use for the transactions you have ed and enter an Additional Reference if required.

Date   28/10/2008   **6**

Additional Reference   Accident during install

Cancel   Help   Back   Next   Finish

Write Off, Refunds and Returns Wizard

Write Off, Refund and Returns

Finished !

Please Check all the information below and click on "Finish" to post this transaction to your ledgers.

Account :   DODGERBO Dodger & Bodger

Date :   28/10/2008

Total :   911.92

Additional Reference: Accident during install   **7**

Cancel   Help   Back   Next   Finish

ALERT: The use of the Write Off, Refunds and Returns Wizard is not recommend where the firm uses VAT cash accounting as the transactions are posted with a tax code which would exclude them from the VAT return.

WHAT DOES THIS MEAN?

There are four types of write-offs:

Write off Customer Accounts: Clears all transactions for the selected customer and would be used where they had gone out of business.

Write off Customer Transactions: Clears selected transactions for one selected customer. Use this where, for whatever reason, an invoice will not be paid.

Write off Customer Transactions below a value: Clears small outstanding transactions for all customers – there is a point below which monies are not worth collecting.

Write off Customer Small Overpayments: Likewise, clears small overpayments, if present, for all customers.

Manage supplier credit

The Credit Control window looks almost the same when opened from the Suppliers module, though it is now called Manage Payments. There is a slightly different set of toolbar buttons here, of course, including this new one – Suggest Payment. If you want to pay several suppliers at the same time, it is simpler to use this routine than the Pay Supplier routine in the Bank module (see page 107).

1 Go to the Supplier module and select the Manage Payments task.

2 Click the Suggest Payment tool to open the Suggested Payments window.

3 Decide how much money you have available and enter this in the Funds for Payment field at the top left. You can allocate funds to suppliers in two ways.

Either:

4 Click Suggest. The funds will be allocated from the top down – paying each supplier in full, as far as possible, then allocating a partial payment with any remaining cash.

Or:

5 Allocate the funds by typing in values or using the calculator.

6 When you have worked out how much to pay each one, click Make Payment.

7 The Supplier Payment window will open, showing the outstanding transactions. You can pay all or a selection of these.

8 To pay a selected transaction, click on it and enter the amount to pay or click Pay in Full to pay the total amount.

9 To pay all transactions fully, click Automatic. Note that if insufficient funds were allocated to this supplier at the earlier stage, the transactions will be paid from the top down until nothing is left.

10 Click Save to record the payments in your files, then select the next supplier from the drop-down Payee list, or click Close to return to the Suggested Payments window.

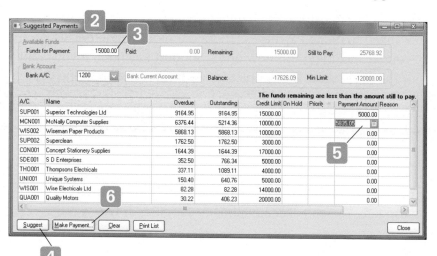

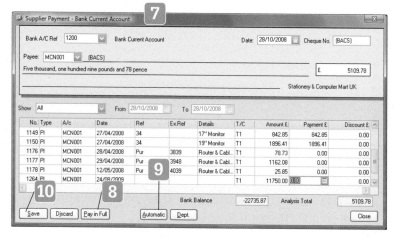

HOT TIP: When entering amounts to pay, if you use the calculator you can also work out how much is left after earlier allocations.

ALERT: The Paid and Remaining values are updated only after you have made the payment – not simply allocated an amount. If you want to know how much is left as you allocate, you have to work it out for yourself – you can use approximate amounts while allocating.

DID YOU KNOW?

The Accountant Plus and Professional versions of Sage 50 Accountant can print your cheques for you.

11 Financial control

Introduction

The Financials window lists all current transactions, which can be useful for tracking things down, but it is also the one-stop access point for the key financial reports, such as the audit trail, trial balance, profit and loss account, balance sheet, and the starting point for preparing for and producing the VAT return, and for running the month-end and year-end routines.

Open the Financials window

The Financials module doesn't appear in the quick access buttons down at the bottom left of the screen, but then, it's not needed on a daily basis as are the Customers, Suppliers, Company, Bank and others. There is, however, a link to it when you are in the Company module, and it can always be reached through the menu system.

1 If it is present, click Financials in the Links. Or ...

2 Click Modules in the Menu bar.

3 Select Financials from the menu.

4 Click on the column headers to sort the list of transactions into different orders, if required.

ALERT: Transactions cannot be viewed or edited from here. If you want anything more than the summary, make a note of the account name and/or Nominal Code, date and transaction number, and use these to locate it in the Customers, Suppliers, Company or Bank modules.

View the Audit Trail

The Audit Trail is a key tool for monitoring and analysing your accounts. It is the record of those transactions that have not yet been fully processed, and those that have been processed but not yet cleared from the system.

The Audit Trail can be viewed, in summary form, in the Financials window. It can be printed out in the same form or in briefer or more detailed forms through the Audit button. The print-out routines also allow you to select the range of transactions by date, number, customer or supplier reference.

1 Click Audit.

2 Select the level of details.

3 Set the Output mode.

4 Click Run.

5 At the Criteria dialogue box, define the range to display, or leave the settings at the defaults to show all current transactions.

6 Click OK.

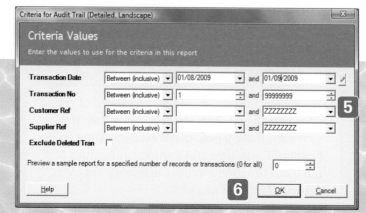

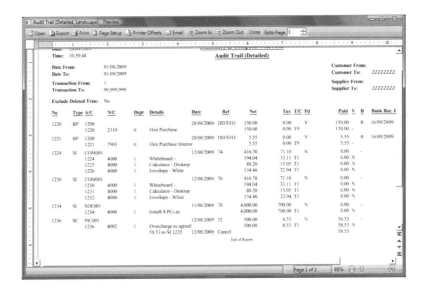

 HOT TIP: The landscape mode works better as there is so much information in each line.

 ALERT: If the auditors want to check your books, they need the Audit Trail (hence the name). If this is not available on the system, it must be available on paper. Make sure that you have a full print-out before running the Clear routine (page 185).

 SEE ALSO: From the Preview window, you can use the Export routine to output the Audit Trail in many formats, including PDF for emailing or printing, XLX or CSV for use in spreadsheets, XML or HTML for use on the Web, and plain text. See page 178.

WHAT DOES THIS MEAN?

These codes are used in the Type column:

BP Bank Payment	BR Bank Receipt
JC Journal Credit	JD Journal Debit
PC Purchase Credit	PI Purchase Invoice
PP Purchase Payment	SA Sale, payment on account
SC Sale, Credit	SI Sale, Invoice
SR Sale Receipt	

Understand a trial balance

The trial balance shows the current debit and credit balance on each account, and the total of all debits and credits. In a manual accounting system, it is used to check that data has been double-entered correctly – the sum of the debit and credit balances should be equal. If they are not, it shows that with at least one transaction, one or both of the values has been entered wrongly or in the wrong column, or has been omitted altogether.

In a Sage system this cannot happen as the value entered for a transaction is automatically posted to two accounts – once as a debit and once as a credit. However, the trial balance is still useful as it gives a convenient summary of the trading figures. If the credit and debit totals didn't balance, it would show that the data had become corrupted.

1 Click Trial.

2 Set the Output mode and click Run.

3 At the Criteria dialogue box, select the end month. If you want just a small sample to check the output style, enter the number of accounts you want to see. Click OK.

The trial balance is based on the data from the start of the year up to a chosen month. Apart from the Output mode, that is your only option.

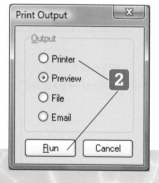

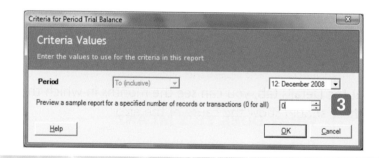

Period Trial Balance

To Period: Month 12, December 2008

N/C	Name	Debit	Credit
0020	Plant and Machinery	50,000.00	
0021	Plant/Machinery Depreciation		3,485.00
0040	Furniture and Fixtures	16,900.00	
0041	Furniture/Fixture Depreciation		93.00
0050	Motor Vehicles	20,300.00	
0051	Motor Vehicles Depreciation		2,091.92
1001	Stock	35,000.00	
1100	Debtors Control Account	75,110.57	
1200	Bank Current Account		19,803.32
1210	Bank Deposit Account	3,510.00	
1220	Building Society Account	507.53	
1230	Petty Cash	1,130.48	
1240	Company Credit Card	9,358.97	
2100	Creditors Control Account		23,681.77
2200	Sales Tax Control Account		22,460.13
2201	Purchase Tax Control Account	12,203.64	
2202	VAT Liability	14,800.35	
2210	P.A.Y.E.		5,396.79
2211	National Insurance		
2230	Pension Fund		
2300	Loans		
2310	Hire Purchase		
3000	Ordinary Shares		
4000	Sales North		
4001	Sales South		
4002	Sales Scotland		
4009	Discounts Allowed		
4400	Credit Charges		
4900	Miscellaneous Income		
4905	Distribution and Carriage		
5000	Materials Purchased		
5001	Materials Imported		
5002	Miscellaneous Purchases		

N/C	Name	Debit	Credit
5009	Discounts Taken		45.00
5100	Carriage	1.26	
5200	Opening Stock	40,710.00	
5201	Closing Stock		35,000.00
6200	Sales Promotions	50.00	
6201	Advertising	465.00	
6202	Gifts and Samples	115.00	
6203	P.R. (Literature & Brochures)	1,050.00	
7000	Gross Wages	32,472.11	
7006	Employers N.I.	3,327.24	
7009	Adjustments	255.00	
7010	SSP Reclaimed	40.00	
7011	SMP Reclaimed	67.60	
7100	Rent	21,000.00	
7200	Electricity	1,252.00	
7300	Fuel and Oil	15.00	
7301	Repairs and Servicing	88.18	
7304	Miscellaneous Motor Expenses	67.50	
7350	Scale Charges	90.27	
7400	Travelling	201.00	
7401	Car Hire	150.00	
7402	Hotels	720.00	
7403	U.K. Entertainment	5.50	
7500	Printing	54.10	
7501	Postage and Carriage		21.50
7502	Telephone	178.72	
7504	Office Stationery	55.00	
7802	Laundry	50.00	
7901	Bank Charges	5.56	
7903	Loan Interest Paid	105.45	
8003	Vehicle Depreciation	1,009.92	
8100	Bad Debt Write Off	911.93	
8222	Bank Interest Received		2.50
9999	Mispostings Account	155.00	
	Totals:	**419,877.89**	**419,877.89**

The trial balance shown here was produced using the demo data – any real one would have a lot more to it than this. Notice that the Mispostings Account shows a balance of £155.00. This has been mis-recorded somewhere along the line and should be investigated. If you open the Mispostings Account in the Company module and look at the Details tab, you can see the months in which the balance appeared – examining those should show the cause of the error.

View the Profit and Loss account

One of the main uses of the information in your accounts is to assess the profitability of your business – and to find ways to make it more profitable. The Profit and Loss account is a key tool for this. It shows the totals of those accounts that are most directly related to trading, and from these it calculates the current stock levels and the gross and net profit.

With the Profit and Loss account, you define the period, allowing you to examine a month or quarter at any point of the year. You can also select the chart of accounts, if you have set up one or more of your own (see page 81 for more on creating charts of accounts).

1 Click P and L in the toolbar of the Financials window.

2 Set the Output mode and click Run.

3 At the Criteria dialogue box, select the months to include From and To.

4 If there are several chart of accounts layouts, select the one to use.

5 Click OK.

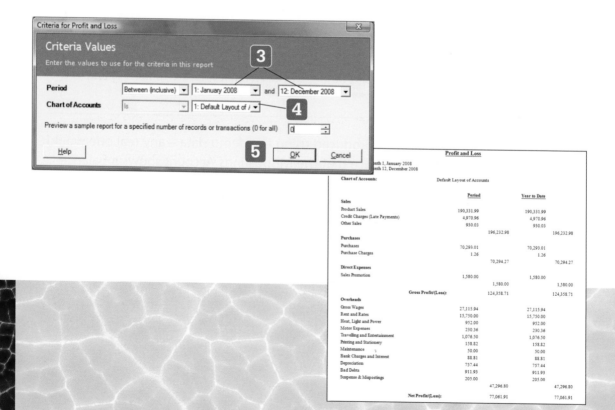

Even if you are scrupulous about entering all sales and costs as they occur, your end-of-period accounts may not give a true picture of the business. Some accounts must be adjusted to reflect the reality of the situation. Stock valuation and depreciation must obviously be handled, and when does a debt become a bad debt?

Another problem is that the expenses entered into the accounts may not relate to the period in question. A business may well pay in arrears for some things and in advance for others. In accounting, these are called accruals and prepayments.

Accruals are monies owing for expenses. Rent, rates, power and phone bills are typically paid in arrears. Even if they are paid on receipt, they are unlikely to coincide exactly with the business's year end. The double-entry solution is to set up an Accruals account and to credit end-of-year bills to this, debiting the matching expense. The true total amount of the expense can then be carried into the Profit and Loss account.

A similar **prepayments** account can be used in the same way, with debits and credits reversed, to handle prepaid bills.

WHAT DOES THIS MEAN?

Gross profit: The difference between your sales income and the cost of goods or raw materials plus the labour and other expenses directly incurred in making and selling the goods.

Direct Expenses: Costs incurred in making sales, i.e. marketing, commission, etc., which will vary in line with sales.

Overheads: The costs incurred in running the business – no matter how much you sell.

Net profit/(loss): Gross profit minus office costs and other general overheads.

Understand a balance sheet

The balance sheet provides a summary of the assets and liabilities of a business. The two totals must balance or there is something wrong with the calculations! The balance sheet – and the budget and prior year outputs – have the same options as the Profit and Loss account.

1 Click Balance.

2 Set the Output mode and click Run.

3 At the Criteria dialogue box, select the months to include From and To.

4 If there are several chart of accounts layouts, select the one to use.

5 Click OK.

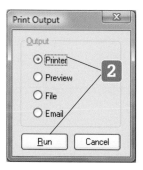

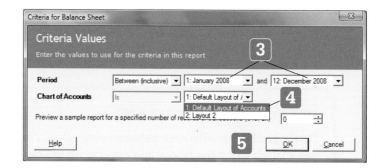

WHAT DOES THIS MEAN?

Fixed assets: Items which have been bought to be retained within the business (for at least a year) and not for resale at a profit. They include equipment, vehicles, property, etc. Any depreciation – or appreciation in value – is entered into the accounts at the end of the period so that a realistic value is present in the balance sheet.

Current assets: Those which should be realised (turned into cash) during the year's trading. They are listed in the balance sheet in order of liquidity, with the least liquid at the top.

Current liabilities: The short-term debts owed by the business – principally, the bank overdraft, suppliers' bills not yet paid, and any wages that are due at that point.

Long-term liabilities: Loans, mortgages and other debts which will be paid off in instalments over time.

Capital and reserves: Include share capital and investment by the owner(s). The profit also sits here until it is distributed to the owners or shareholders, or is reinvested in the business.

ALERT: You can draw a crucial measure from the current assets and liabilities figures. The **Liquidity ratio** shows whether a business can find the cash it needs to meet its short-term debts. It is calculated by the simple formula:

$$\text{Liquidity Ratio} = \frac{\text{Current Assets}}{\text{Current Liabilities}}$$

If the ratio is less than 1.0, the business is in trouble. In the Sage balance sheet display, the Current Assets less Liabilities figure gives a similar guide – this should be a positive value.

Balance Sheet

From: Month 1, January 2008
To: Month 12, December 2008

Chart of Account: Default Layout of Accounts

	Period		Year to Date	
Fixed Assets				
Plant and Machinery	515.00		46,515.00	
Furniture and Fixtures	0.00		16,807.00	
Motor Vehicles	(757.44)		18,208.08	
		(242.44)		81,530.08
Current Assets				
Stock	0.00		35,000.00	
Debtors	72,851.12		75,110.57	
Deposits and Cash	(2,529.62)		(720.12)	
VAT Liability	3,472.82		4,543.86	
		73,794.32		113,934.31
Current Liabilities				
Creditors : Short Term	9,833.93		17,813.64	
Taxation	3,073.72		7,403.77	
Wages	80.00		120.00	
Credit Card (Creditors)	(10,414.97)		(9,358.97)	
Bank Account	3,529.49		27,010.52	
		6,102.17		42,988.96
Current Assets less Current Liabilities:		67,692.15		70,945.35
Total Assets less Current Liabilities:		67,449.71		152,475.43
Long Term Liabilities				
Creditors : Long Term	(2,405.00)		13,055.00	
		(2,405.00)		13,055.00
Total Assets less Total Liabilities:		69,854.71		139,420.43
Capital & Reserves				
Share Capital	0.00		96,332.00	
P&L Account	69,854.71		69,854.71	
Previous Year Adj			(26,766.28)	
		69,854.71		139,420.43

SEE ALSO: If the layout of the balance sheet doesn't suit your business, use a different chart of accounts or design your own. See pages 35 and 81.

Output to file

Any of these financial reports can be output to file for analysis or other uses elsewhere. The export options are:

- PDF (Portable Document Format) can be emailed and viewed on screen, or printed on any printer.

- XML and HTML can be viewed by web browsers.

- RTF (Rich Text Format) and TXT are formatted and plain text files that can be read by any word processor.

- XLS is the Excel spreadsheet format – some routines also offer XLSX, for Excel 2007 and later.

- CSV (Comma Separated Values) is for use with other spreadsheet systems and databases.

- BMP (BitMaP) is an image which could be inserted into a printed report or a presentation.

- Datareport is Sage's own data report format.

- PRN is a printer file for a specific printer – useful if your normal printer is temporarily offline.

1 When you click a button to create any report, the Print Output dialogue box opens. Select File and click Run.

2 The Save As dialogue box will open. Set the Save in folder and File name as usual, then drop down the Save as type list and select a suitable format.

3 Click Save.

Verify your files

The verification routines can be used to check your data before you run the VAT Return. There are four possible routines.

1 Click Verify.

2 At the Verify System dialogue box, select the type of verification.

3 You may need to define this more closely – if you have a lot of transactions, it may be better to look at only one thing at a time.

4 Set the date range and click OK.

5 Click Print for a hard copy of the list to use for reference.

6 Close the window when you've finished, or use the tab to switch back to the Financials display.

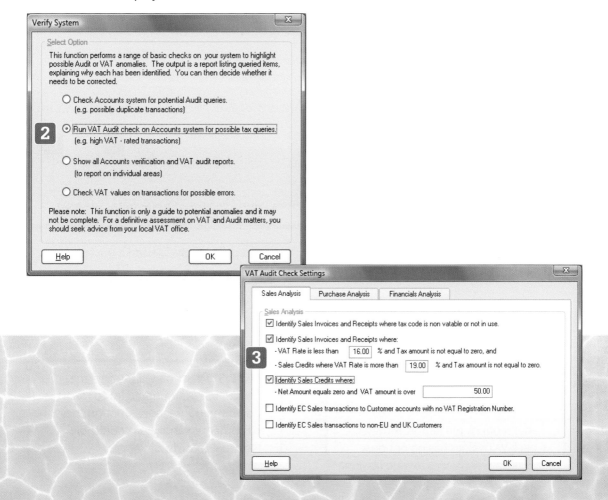

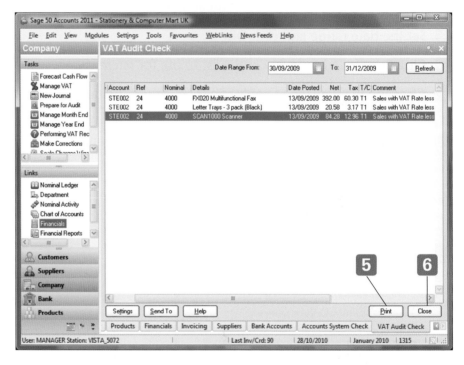

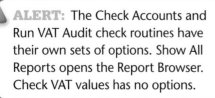

ALERT: The Check Accounts and Run VAT Audit check routines have their own sets of options. Show All Reports opens the Report Browser. Check VAT values has no options.

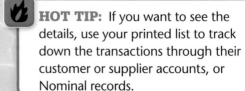

HOT TIP: If you want to see the details, use your printed list to track down the transactions through their customer or supplier accounts, or Nominal records.

Make the VAT return

I like the way VAT is handled – for two reasons. First, Sage 50 does all the work for you! And second, the window follows the design of the standard VAT form, just as the payments screen mimics a cheque, and that makes transferring figures a breeze.

1 Click the VAT button to open the VAT Return window.

2 Set the period start and end in the fields at the top right.

3 If you want to Include Reconciled transactions, tick the box.

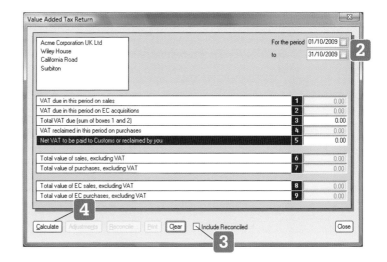

4 Click Calculate. If there are also unreconciled transactions, you will be told and can choose whether to include them.

5 If you need to adjust any of the figures, e.g. to correct earlier under- or overpayments, click Adjustments and enter the figures there.

6 If you want a report, click Print.

 HOT TIP: You should work through the VAT options in the Verify routine before you run the VAT return to ensure that your records are fully up to date and correct.

? DID YOU KNOW?

Calculating VAT has no effect on your data, so you can do it as often as need be – e.g. you may want to run it early to get an idea of the likely amount to pay. Once you have done the final calculation for a period, click Reconcile to mark the items as processed so that they do not appear in future returns.

7 Select the VAT Return Type and the Output mode.

8 Click Run.

9 Click OK when you've finished.

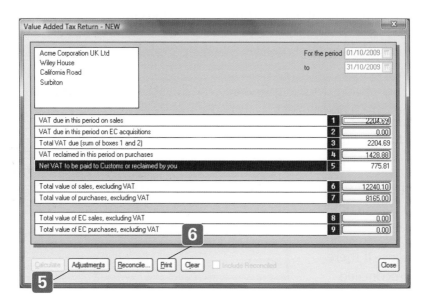

Manage the month end

The month end routines are optional. Their purpose is to handle recurring entries, update stock and asset valuations and tidy up the customer and supplier accounts so that you don't have to wade through old data, but to do this without losing essential information. They take time to run, but could save time overall. Look closely at your accounts and talk to your accountant.

There are four main stages to the operation. The initial Welcome screen simply outlines the process. The later screens take you through a series of jobs, with direct links to each operation.

1 In the Financials or the Company module, select Manage Month End in the Tasks pane. The Period End window will open. Navigate through it by clicking on the links on the left.

2 In the Preparation stage you tidy up the accounts for the month.

3 Click to post current transactions.

4 Click to process recurring entries.

5 Click to update the stock and make journal entries, e.g. prepayments and accruals, depreciation, etc.

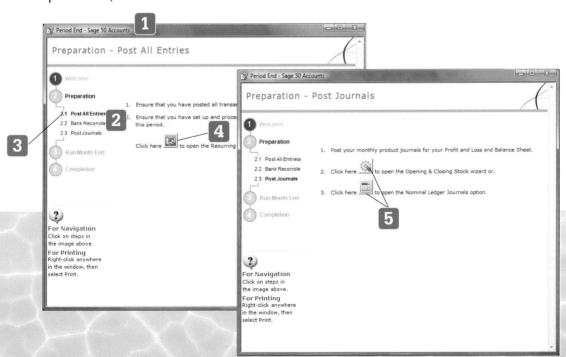

6 At the Run Month End stage, you will be prompted to make a backup, so have your backup media ready. After setting the program date to the month-end date, the month-end procedure is run.

7 At the Month End dialogue box, there are four options – check those which are relevant and click OK.

8 At the Completion stage you can clear the Audit Trail.

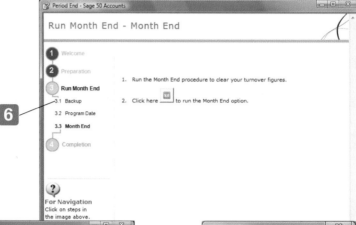

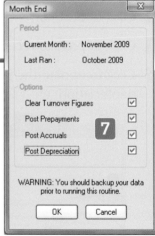

ALERT: Some of these may not be relevant to your business or the way you handle your accounts (e.g. do you need to calculate depreciation on your fixed assets monthly?).

? DID YOU KNOW?

In the Month End options, Clear Turnover Figures resets Customer and Supplier monthly turnover figures to 0. Post Prepayments and Post Accruals will process prepayments or accruals if any have been set up.

Clear the Audit Trail

Clearing removes all those transactions that have been fully paid, reconciled with the bank statement and processed for the VAT return. As it does so, it calculates the effect of the transactions on the accounts and rewrites the opening balances.

Before you start you must have hard copies of all your transactions. Print the reports for the Audit Trail, Monthly Day Books, Sales, Purchase and Nominal Activity and VAT Return. You must also have backed up your data.

1 Start the Clear Audit Trail Wizard from the final stage of the Month End routine.

2 Read the prompts and warnings as you work through the wizard. At the third stage, enter the date to clear up to – this will typically be the last month end.

3 When the wizard has finished, you will be offered a chance to view the cleared transactions. View them and print the report for your records. You cannot be too careful with your data.

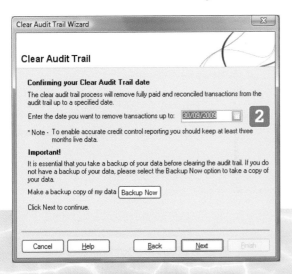

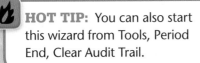

HOT TIP: You can also start this wizard from Tools, Period End, Clear Audit Trail.

HOT TIP: How long you keep transactions in the Audit Trail is for you and your accountant to decide. The Sage 50 system is capable of storing up to 2 billion transactions, so space is not an issue (as long as your hard disk is big enough and your backup media can cope with the file sizes). Speed – or rather the lack of it – may become an issue, as response time can slow down with very large files. Normal practice is for the Audit Trail to be cleared as part of your regular end-of-period routines.

Manage the year end

The Year End routine follows the same patterns as that of the Month End – its main purpose is to transfer summary figures to the 'Prior Year', ready for the start of the new financial year. The Month End routine for month 12 can be done immediately before this, or as part of its first stage.

1 Select Manage Year End in the Tasks pane. The Period End window will open. Click the links on the left to work through it, and click the icons in the main area to go back into the system to run backups, printing and other operations.

2 Every part of the Preparation stage is essential (unless the Month End has been done already). To check the Chart of Accounts you need to go back into the system and run the check from the Company module.

3 The Year End phase has only one operation. Click the button to perform the Year End postings. This moves the current balances to opening balances on all accounts.

4 At the Year End dialogue box, select the Output mode – Printer or File.

5 If you use the budgeting facilities, tick the options to transfer the actual figures to the budgets and to generate next year's budgets (setting increases if appropriate).

6 Double check that you have all the necessary backups and print-outs, and if you have, click OK to run the routine.

7 The final stages of the Year End procedure are about tidying up – clearing old data and removing accounts which are no longer in use.

ALERT: Backups and print-outs to secure old data are key parts of this procedure, so have your backup media and paper ready.

SEE ALSO: If your check of the Chart of Accounts shows errors, they can usually be solved with some simple editing. See Edit the Chart of Accounts, page 81.

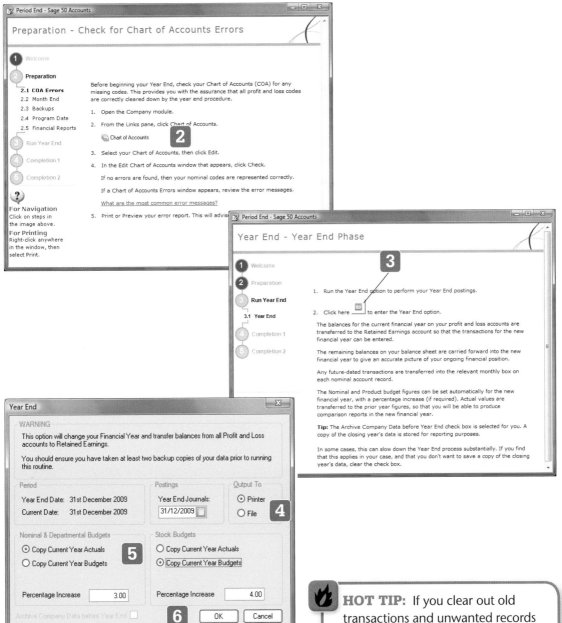

ALERT: Many of the year-end routines are optional, but recommended. They are mainly about removing redundant accounts or records of past transactions. A tidy system should run a little faster and is simpler to use.

HOT TIP: If you clear out old transactions and unwanted records – as you normally should – use the Compress Data option at the last stage. When a record is deleted, it leaves a hole in the file that it was stored in. Compression reorganises the file to close up the holes. A smaller file takes up less space on the disk, loads in faster and is read more quickly.

12 Products

Introduction

The Products module provides stock control facilities, but the product information is also used when generating invoices and credit notes – selecting a product's code will pull in its description, price, tax rate and default order quantity. It can take time to enter the details of all your business's products, but it will save more time in the long run. You can speed up data entry by setting appropriate defaults for the products.

If you have a large inventory, maintaining full, accurate product and price lists can be quite time consuming, but it delivers faster, more efficient invoicing and should save much more time in the long run.

Explore the Products window

The tools in this window let you create new product records, edit existing records, update stock levels, maintain price lists and print the information.

 Create a new product record.

2 View or edit a product record.

3 Show movement of selected products.

4 Record movements of stock in and out.

5 Run the stock taking routine.

ALERT: The Closing Stock wizard will write the stock value into the Stock and Closing Stock nominal accounts.

SEE ALSO: Before you do any work on your products, check and set the defaults – see page 193.

Create categories

Products can be organised into categories. If you sell through a website, these can help your customers to locate items. Categories can also be useful for analysing your business activities.

If you intend to use categories, they are best created before setting the defaults and before entering the details of products.

1 Open the Settings menu, select Configuration and switch to the Products panel.

2 Select an unused category and click Edit.

3 Enter a name and click OK.

4 Repeat for all your new categories, then click Apply to store the definitions in your configuration data, or Save to save the new configuration to file.

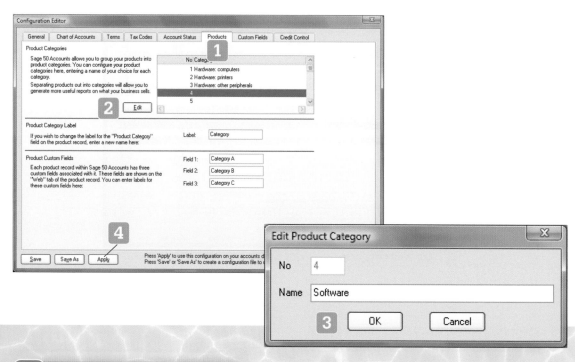

HOT TIP: If necessary, a new product category can be set up when you are creating a product record.

Set product defaults

A well-thought-out set of product defaults can speed up the creation of records. Spend a few moments before you start working out what are the most common settings for Nominal Code, Tax Code, Unit of Sale – as single units, or in packs of ten (or whatever) – Category and Department. You also need to think about decimal precision – are the quantities mainly whole units or sold by weight or volume, measured to what accuracy?

1 Open the Settings menu and select Product Defaults.

2 Set suitable values for Nominal Code, Tax Code, Unit of Sale, Category and Department.

3 Set the number of decimal places to show for Quantities and Prices on invoices.

4 Click OK.

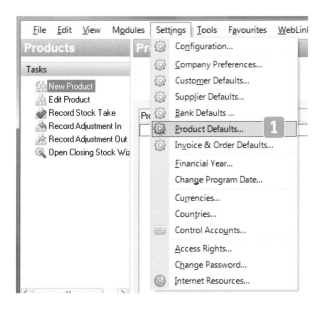

WHAT DOES THIS MEAN?

In the Decimal Precision area:

Quantity D.P.: Refers to the number of decimal places to show for quantity in invoices.

Unit D.P.: Refers to the pricing units – leave it at 2 for prices in pounds and pence or euros and cents.

Create product records

New product records are set up through a wizard. This will ask for a range of details. If you do not know some of them at the time, enter them later by editing the product record.

1 In the Product window, click New.

2 Click Next to get past the first page and enter a Description. The Code will be created for you. Click Next.

3 Enter the Location, Category and other details if required. Click Next.

4 Enter the Sale Price and change the Sales Nominal Code, Unit of Sale, Tax Code and Department if the defaults do not suit. Click Next.

5 Select the Supplier A/C and enter the Part No., Re-Order Level and Quantity and Cost Price if required. Click Next.

6 You will be asked whether you want to set an opening balance. If you do, select Yes, then enter the Reference, Date, Quantity and Cost Price – this is the price per unit, not the total. Click Next.

7 Click Finish to save the product data.

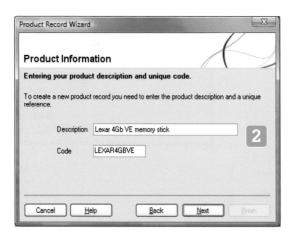

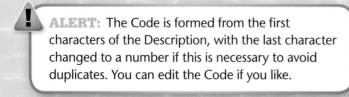

ALERT: The Code is formed from the first characters of the Description, with the last character changed to a number if this is necessary to avoid duplicates. You can edit the Code if you like.

 ALERT: Before you can use the product record properly, it must have the Description, Code, Sale Price, Tax Code, Unit of Sale and Nominal Code.

 HOT TIP: Not all of these product details may be relevant to your business. Don't waste time entering useless information.

View and edit product data

The product records contain the information that you entered when you created them, plus details of any sales or other stock movements. There is also a Memo tab for any notes you wish to add and a Web tab which can hold images and text for use in webpages.

If prices or other details have changed, or if there are errors or omissions in your product data, the records are easily edited.

1 Select the record(s) you want to edit.

2 Click Record.

3 Edit the record. Add details to the Memo tab if required.

4 Click Save.

5 Click Next if there are more records, or select a new record from the Product Code at the top left and repeat steps 2 to 4.

6 Click Close.

ALERT: When you are creating an invoice, if you find that a product is not on the system, click the New button on the Products list. A Product Record window will open to collect essential details.

DID YOU KNOW?
In Accountant Plus and Professional the Product record has a BOM (bill of materials) tab, where the components of a compound product can be listed. The cost of the compound product is calculated for you from those of its components.

Use price lists

The Accountant Plus and Professional versions of Sage 50 have a useful price list facility. This can be a great timesaver if you sell products at different prices according to the nature of the customer – as opposed to, or as well as, giving discounts to categories of customers.

1 Click the Prices button on the toolbar.

2 At the Price Lists window, click New.

3 You will be asked which type of price list you wish to create. Click Customer.

4 At the Edit Price List window, enter a Name and a Description for the list.

5 Click Add to add the first product to the list. (The window will change its title to Edit Price List.)

6 At the Add Products dialogue box, select an item from the list.

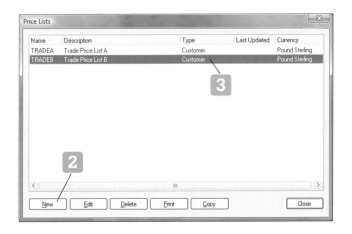

 HOT TIP: Supplier lists are much the same, but a little simpler.

? DID YOU KNOW?
A price list has two aspects: the products and their prices, and the customers to whom those prices apply. If price lists exist, when you add a product to an invoice Sage 50 will check the lists to see which price to use for the customer. If the customer is not on any list, the standard price will be applied.

7 The Set pricing method values determine how the product's price is calculated for the list. It can be a fixed price, or vary from the cost price by a percentage or by a value.

8 Click OK to add the product and its price to the list.

9 Click Save and repeat steps 5 to 7 for the other products.

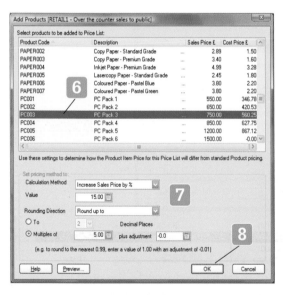

 ALERT: If you use percentages to set prices for this list, this can produce fractional amounts, but these can be rounded up or down. You can also work in multiples with an adjustment, e.g. whole pounds minus 1p to give 3.99, 6.99 prices.

HOT TIP: The Set pricing method settings can be changed for individual products, though you would normally apply the same adjustment across the board, or across types of products.

Add customers to a price list

You can add selected customers to a list so that its prices are applied when they place an order. This is going to be of most use with lists for trade customers.

1 Open the price list.

2 Switch to the Customers tab.

3 Click Add.

4 Select a customer to whom the price will apply. Click OK.

5 Repeat steps 3 and 4 to add all the relevant customers.

6 Click Save and Close.

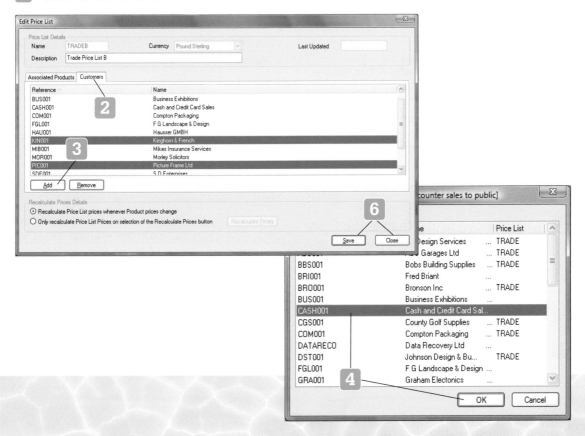

 ALERT: Notice that if a customer is already on a list, this is shown in the right-hand column.

 HOT TIP: If you later want to remove a customer from a list, simply select the name and click Remove.

Adjust stock levels

The Products records can be used to keep track of stock levels. You can enter the quantities in stock when first setting up a record or after a stock take. If goods are sold via invoices, the movements out are automatically marked on the product record when the invoice is posted. Deliveries, non-invoiced sales and other movements are handled through the routines in the Products module:

- In (adjustment in) – deliveries and returns.

- Out (adjustment out) – sales and losses.

- Stock Take – updating the files after a manual stock take.

1 Select the products to be adjusted. This is not essential as products can be selected at step 3, but it may be simpler to select them all at the start.

2 Click In or Out.

3 Select the Product Code, if necessary.

4 The Date will be set to the program date. Adjust if necessary.

5 Enter a Ref and/or Project Ref if required.

6 Enter the Quantity.

7 With In movements, change the Cost Price if it is different from the default.

8 Repeat steps 3 to 7 for other products.

9 Click Save.

10 Click Close.

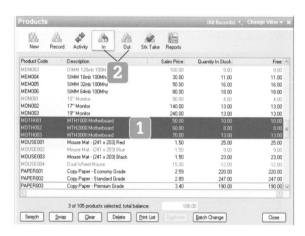

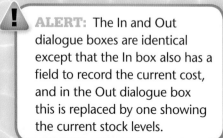

ALERT: The In and Out dialogue boxes are identical except that the In box also has a field to record the current cost, and in the Out dialogue box this is replaced by one showing the current stock levels.

Take stock

In a perfect world, the stock adjustments through the invoicing and the In and Out routines should mean that the numbers in stock according to the system should be the same as the number actually on the shelves and in the storerooms. In this imperfect world, goods get lost, stolen, mislaid or dropped and broken. Regular stock taking is necessary to keep your records in line with reality.

1 Select the products, or leave this until step 3.

2 Click the Stock Take button.

3 Select the Product Code, if necessary.

4 Adjust the Date if necessary.

5 Enter the Actual number in stock.

6 Repeat steps 3 to 5 for other products.

7 Click Save, then Close.

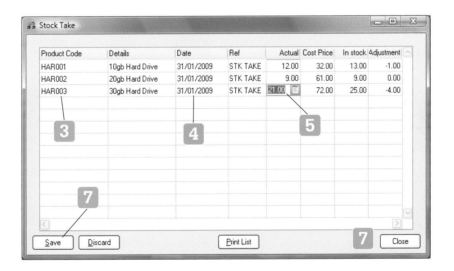

ALERT: If the owner doesn't take stock, the employees may.

13 Help and support

Introduction

Sage 50 systems have many features. Some of these you may never use, as they are not applicable to your business, others will be used only rarely, at year ends or when particular problems arise. So, though you will soon be at ease with the routine chores – most of which should be covered in this book – there will be times when you find yourself saying, 'How do I do this?' At times like this, turn first to the Help pages. To find information, you can browse through the Contents, look it up in the Index or Search for it.

If the Help pages alone do not provide the answer, there is more information, technical support and other types of help available online at Sage's website (www.sage.co.uk).

Get help through the Contents

The Contents panel offers the best approach when you are looking for help with a module or operation. Here, the Help pages are organised into sections, with two or three levels of subdivisions. If the first page that you find does not tell you quite what you want to know, look for the links to related pages and follow these up to find the answer.

1 Open the Help menu and click Contents and Index.

2 If necessary, click the Contents tab.

3 Click [+] to open a section. Most have subsections – click a second level [+] to reach the pages.

4 Click on an item to display its page in the main pane.

5 If the display is getting crowded, click the [–] icons to close up unwanted branches.

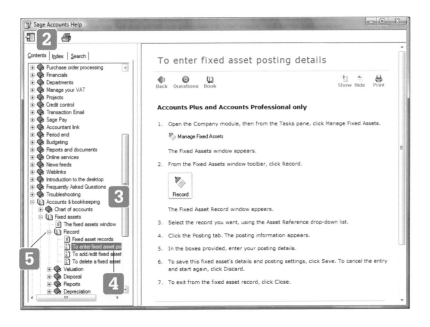

HOT TIP: Most of the Help pages are organised around the different modules, tools and features of the Sage system – as you would expect – but sometimes you may not know where in the system you should start to look for help. At times like these, the Frequently Asked Questions can be very useful.

? DID YOU KNOW?
If you need explanations of accountancy terms, look in the Glossary – it's down at the bottom of the list.

Navigate a Help page

There are two sets of tools in the Help system. At the very top, on the frame, are four:

- Show/Hide opens or closes the left-hand pane – you may need the screen space.

- The Back and Forward arrows take you to other pages you have viewed in the session.

- The Printer icon will print the page.

The second set of tools is on the page itself.

- Back takes you back to the last page you were looking at.

- Questions takes you to the Frequently Asked Questions page for the topic, where you will find answers to many of your queries.

- Book takes you to a 'Book' page, which holds a set of links to related topics.

- Show All displays all the drop-down text or hidden images (see below) on the page.

- Hide all closes up all drop-down text and images.

- Print sends the current page to the printer.

Any text in cyan (blue–green) is a link.

- If the text is underlined, clicking on it will take you to a linked page.

- If it is not underlined, clicking on it will drop down an explanation of the term or display a hidden image, e.g. a screenshot. Click again to hide it.

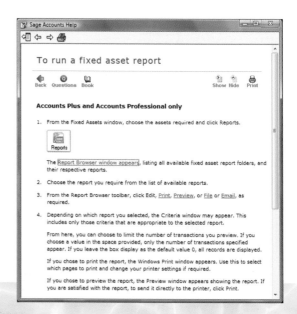

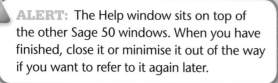

ALERT: The Help window sits on top of the other Sage 50 windows. When you have finished, close it or minimise it out of the way if you want to refer to it again later.

Use the Index

The Index contains nearly 2,500 entries and subentries, in alphabetical order. You can scroll through to find an entry, but it is quicker to type in the first few letters of a word and jump to the relevant part of the Index. Most entries lead to a single page, but sometimes you will be offered a choice of pages from the same word.

If you were using the Index when you last shut down Help, the Contents and Index option will reopen Help at the Index.

1 Open the Help menu and select Contents and Index.

2 If necessary, click the Index tab.

3 Drag the slider to scroll through the Index.

4 Type the first few letters of the word to jump to the right part of the list.

5 Double-click on an entry or select it and click Display.

6 If the Topics Found panel opens to offer you a choice, select one and click Display.

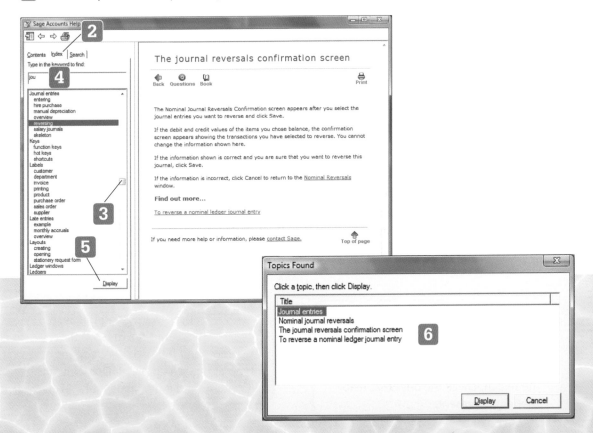

Search for help

A search hunts through the entire text of the Help system. It normally produces more results, as it will find every page containing a given word, not just the main ones on the topic. This can be useful as you can get a more thorough understanding of an issue by following up all the leads, but if all you want to do is find the meaning of a word, or learn how to do a particular job, it can take a bit longer to locate the relevant page.

1 Open the Help menu or click the Help button and select Contents and Index.

2 If necessary, click the Search tab.

3 Type one or more words to define the Help you need.

4 Click List Topics.

5 Select a topic from the bottom pane.

6 Click Display.

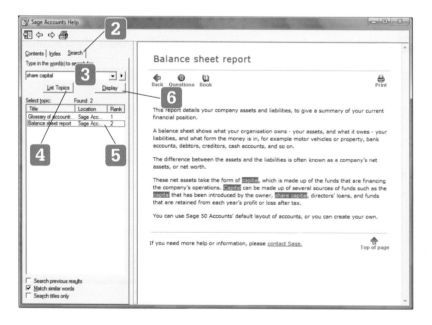

HOT TIP: The searches find all pages which contain any or all of the search words. These will be highlighted in the page. If you have used several words in the search, check the ones that really matter are present.

ALERT: If you were using the Search when you last shut down Help, the Contents and Index option reopens Help at the Search panel. Don't let 'Contents and Index' fool you!

Get help online

The options on the WebLinks menu connect you to the Internet and take you to Sage's website. Browsing through the site, you will find mainly news and information about Sage's products and services, along with some good articles on major topics. If you are looking for in-depth answers to more complex questions, you should head to the Ask Sage area, but to get there you need to subscribe to SageCover.

SageCover gives you access, via email or phone, to additional expert advice and assistance with Sage systems and with accountancy and other aspects of business in general. It is free for the first six weeks after purchasing Sage software. Continuing cover can be bought online from the Sage shop. The cost varies depending upon the software, the number of users and the level of support required.

1 Open the WebLinks menu and select Sage Home Page.

2 At the home page, click the Support and Training link.

3 At Ask Sage, type some words to define what you are looking for in the Search text box.

4 Click Search.

5 Click on an article's title to read it. It will open in a new window.

ALERT: Before you can get into the SageCover members' areas, you need to register with Sage. For this you will need your account number or the serial number of your software. Dig out the box – it's in there. Once you have registered, you can log in and use the members' areas.

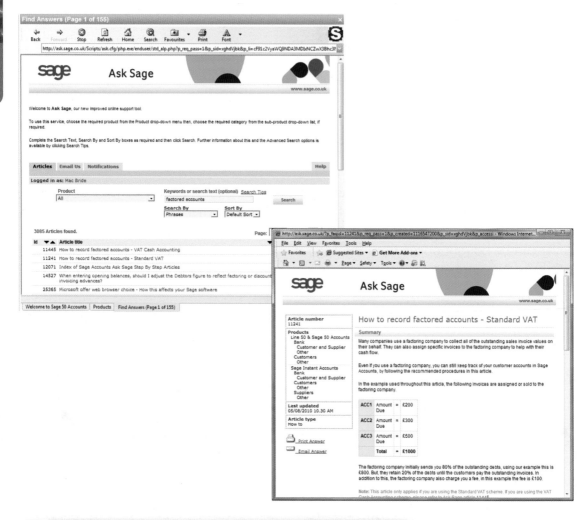

 HOT TIP: There are more than 10,000 articles in the Ask Sage database. Asking very specific questions can help to locate the right information, but sometimes it is better to use only a single keyword and then browse the results. You will see that some are 'step by step' to walk you through a process, while others are classed as 'definitions and summaries'.

 ALERT: If you can't find an answer in the Knowledgebase, go to Ask Support and email your problem to the support staff.

Top 10 Sage Accounting Problems Solved

Problem 1: It says I'm already logged on – but I haven't started yet!

The trouble is, you didn't log off properly last time. This may have been because of a computer crash, or a fault in shutting down, or with a newly installed system because you have not yet set the Access Rights. To solve the problem you need to delete the temporary file created by Sage to record your logon. Its location depends upon the Windows version.

1 Open the Help menu and select About.

2 Bring the System Information tab to the front.

3 Select Directories in the left pane.

4 Make a note of the path to the data files. In this case it is C:\ProgramData\Sage\ Accounts.

5 Open Computer (or My Computer or Windows Explorer).

6 In the folder list, select the C: drive and navigate to the Accounts folder.

7 Open the Accounts, then 2011, then the folder for the data you had been using – Company, Demodata or Practice.

8 Open the folder ACCDATA.

9 List the files in date order, with the newest at the top.

10 Close to the top of the list you will see QUEUE.DTA. Right-click on it and select Delete.

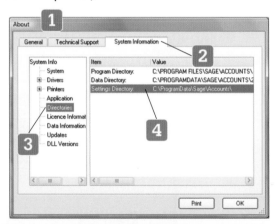

Problem 2: I've sold something we no longer have, so the invoice is wrong

There are two possible solutions here. If the invoice has not yet been updated into the ledgers and sent to the customer, you can edit it easily.

1 Go to the Invoice List window.

2 Locate the invoice and double-click on it, or select it and click New/Edit.

3 On the line for the item, click into each of these cells in turn and press the Delete key to erase the contents: Product Code, Description, Quantity and Price. The Net and VAT cells will be cleared automatically.

4 Click Save.

5 Click Close.

SEE ALSO: If the invoice has been posted, you will need to create a credit note for the unavailable item. See Create a credit note, page 142.

Problem 3: I hate those mice! Can I work from the keyboard?

The Sage system is simplest to operate under mouse control, but you can work with just the keyboard if you have to, or if you prefer. Some things can be done using the normal Windows techniques; some are special to Sage; most need practice.

To access the menu system:

1 Press Alt, then press an underlined key to open its menu, or use the arrow keys to move around the menus.

To run an operation from a button at the bottom of the screen:

2 Press Alt + the underlined letter on the button at the same time. Or …

3 Press Tab until the button is selected, then press Enter.

To switch to another open tab:

4 Press Ctrl + Tab.

To select a toolbar button:

5 Press Tab until the first of the buttons is highlighted – you have to work through the lower set of buttons first – then press the space bar.

Problem 4: They've gone bust! How do I write off what they owe us?

Write-offs start at the Write Off button in the Task list of the Customer module or the Chase Debt window. There's a wizard to walk you through the process, which makes it all quite straightforward.

1 Click the Customer Write Off/Refund task or the Write Off toolbar button.

2 At the Write Off, Refunds and Returns Wizard, select Write off Customer Accounts.

3 Click Next.

4 Select the customer. Click Next.

5 At the next stage you will be shown which transactions will be written off – you cannot change anything here.

6 Set the date and add a reference for the operation. Click Next.

7 At the final stage, the details collected by the wizard will be shown. Click Finish to post the write-off.

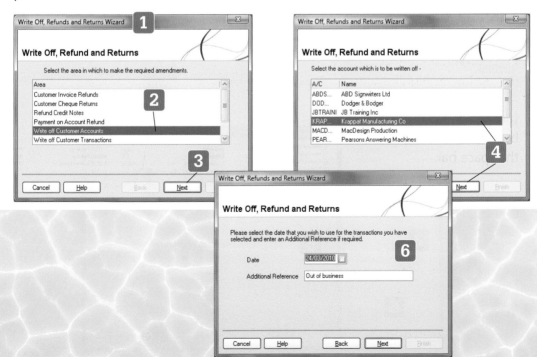

Problem 5: The trial balance shows depreciation in the same column as the asset. That can't be right, can it?

No, it can't. Someone has attempted to record depreciation by journal entries and has got it the wrong way round. There are two Nominal accounts to record the depreciation of each type of asset – one up at the top in the Balance Sheet area and one down at the bottom in the Profit and Loss area. The depreciation charge should go into the Balance Sheet as a credit and into the Profit and Loss account as a debit. To correct it, you should first reverse the misposting, then write it in properly.

1 Go to the Company module and display the Nominal Ledger.

2 Select the two depreciation accounts – one will have an N/C of under 100, the other around 8000. Note the value of the charge.

3 In the low number, Balance Sheet account, write the Details as 'Correction', or something similar, and enter the amount as a Credit.

4 In the 8000+ Profit and Loss account, write the same Details description and enter the value as a Debit.

5 Repeat steps 3 and 4, but with the Details as 'Annual Depreciation' or something similar.

6 Click Save, then Close.

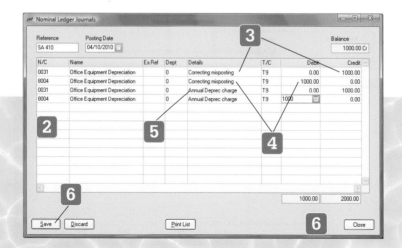

Problem 6: The computer is dead/stolen/waterlogged. What do I do?

First thing, don't panic. As long as you have been making backups regularly and keeping them safe, you can get back to normal fairly quickly.

1 Go and buy a new computer – it's rarely worth thinking about a repair unless it's quite new and still under guarantee.

2 Install the Sage software.

3 Find the disk, tape, external hard drive or memory stick with the latest backup.

4 Run Sage and select Open Company Data. The Company Set-up Wizard will run. Select the Restore data option.

5 You will need to reactivate Sage with the serial number and activation key.

6 At the Select Back-up File stage, click Browse and locate the file. Click Next.

7 Wait while the files are copied back into place. While this is happening, locate the paperwork and any other records of the transactions that have taken place since the last backup.

8 Re-enter the missing transactions to get back up to date.

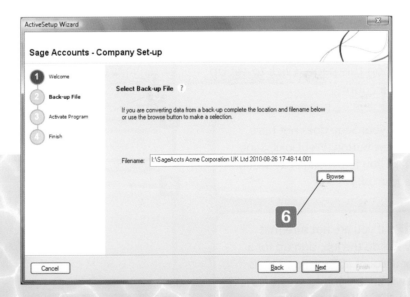

Problem 7: I've started selling online. Should I use Sage Pay to collect payments?

Why not? It's a well-developed, secure service that can be implemented in different ways to suit your business and the structure and nature of your website. If you are already selling online, you should have in place already most of what you need to set up a Sage Pay account.

1 Open the Settings, Company Preferences dialogue box.

2 Switch to the Sage Pay window and tick Enable Sage Pay.

3 Type in your company's name and contact information in the Credentials area.

4 Set the Bank account to receive the money.

5 Tick Check for payments on startup to download payments at the start of each day.

6 Tick Prompt for password on each login to Sage Pay if you want to restrict access to your online account.

7 Payment data can be allocated to individual customers, who are recognised by their email addresses.

8 If you are selling to the general public, it will be simpler to set up a single account to record online sales.

9 Some versions of Sage have an Apply Now button on this page. Click to set up your online account.

ALERT: If your Sage does not have an Apply Now button, WebLinks, Sage Pay will take you to the Sage Pay section (www.sage.co.uk.)

HOT TIP: If you are not sure that Sage Pay will do the job, sign up for a Simulator account at Sage Pay. This is free and will enable you to see how well Sage Pay will work for you.

Problem 8: I need to keep some of the staff out of some of the areas. How do I do that?

If several people work on the accounts, they may not all need access to all areas – the clerk recording sales may not be involved in credit control; junior staff should have no need to create or edit Nominal accounts. Sage lets you control which modules people can access and which dialogues within a module.

1 Open the Settings menu and select Access Rights.

2 Select the user and click Details.

3 Click Modules.

4 Select Full or Partial in the Access Type column.

5 Click OK to save the settings.

6 Click the + sign beside a module to see a list of its dialogues.

7 To set access at this level, select the module, then click Dialogues and set access as for Modules.

8 Click Close.

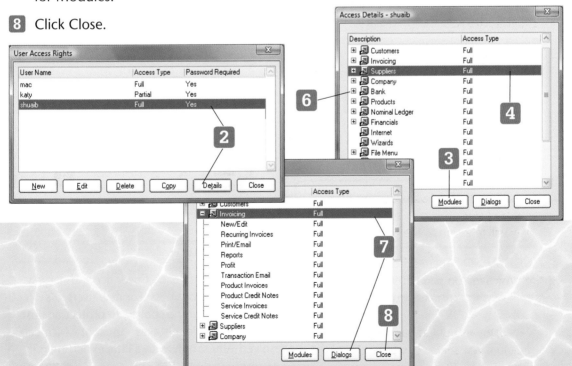

Problem 9: It's a complicated problem and I can't find the answer in the Help pages. Where can I get more help?

Sage offers extensive support services. A basic level of support is available to all registered users, while a comprehensive telephone and online service is offered under the Sage Cover scheme. The Knowledgebase at Ask Sage will provide answers to many questions. If there is a technical problem with the software, you can contact Sage by phone or email. When doing this, it is helpful if you have key details of your software at hand.

1 Open the Help menu and click About.

2 From the General tab, make a note of the version number (e.g. 17.0.12.196) and your registered name and serial number.

3 From the System Information tab, in the Directories section, make a note of where your program, data and settings files are stored.

4 Go to the Technical Support tab to find the phone number or email address.

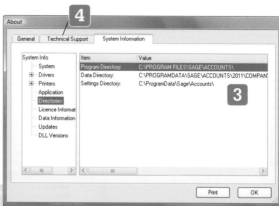

▶ **SEE ALSO:** There's more on Ask Sage on page 209.

! **ALERT:** The cost of Sage Cover depends largely on the size of your business. For new users, it's best seen as an insurance policy, to protect against the almost inevitable mistakes – most of which can be resolved very simply with a little expert help.

Problem 10: I've forgotten my password, again!

As long as you are not the manager, this is not a problem. You just have to go, cap in hand, and ask whoever has 'manager' access to log on and change your password for you.

If you are the manager, it is a real problem. The passwords are stored in an encrypted file and there's no way that you can get into that and read it. You are going to have to contact Sage Technical Support, and they will charge you for decoding the password.

Write it down and keep it somewhere secure, preferably in a safe.

Use your computer with confidence

Office 2010 — 9780273736127

Excel 2010 — 9780273736134

Word 2010 — 9780273736141

Powerpoint 2010 — 9780273736158

Windows 7 — 9780273729136

    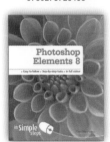

Excel 2007 — 9780273723547

Office 2007 — 9780273723554

Laptop Basics Windows 7 Edition — 9780273736806

Computer Basics Windows 7 edition — 9780273736844

Windows Vista — 9780273723493

Laptop Basics — 9780273723486

Mac Basics — 9780273729297

Computer Basics — 9780273723479

Photoshop CS5 — 9780273736820

Photoshop Elements 8 — 9780273734390

Web Design — 9780273723530

Netbook Basics — 9780273734925

Windows 7 for the Over 50s — 9780273729181

Laptop Basics for the Over 50s — 9780273729129

Computer Basics for the Over 50s — 9780273729174

Practical. Simple. Fast.

PEARSON